MW01007444

Winning the Business Systems Analyst Job Interview

by Kuebiko Global (www.kuebikoglobal.com)

Acknowledgments

We could not have written this book without the encouragement of students and teachers who pushed us to give our best. We were lucky to have incredible trainers (who are also senior industry professionals) who were instrumental in compiling this body of knowledge. Thanks to the hundreds of students we have taught over so many years that helped us by sharing feedback on their interview experiences. We also acknowledge and appreciate the role that our clients, families, and friends played in making this book a reality.

But our deepest gratitude goes to readers like you for purchasing this book. Thank you. We at Kuebiko Global wish you a happy journey and a very successful career as a business systems analyst.

A Letter to the Reader

Dear friend,

This book is intended to help you in many ways. However, the fundamental objective is very simple – to help job seekers clear the interview process and land a job as a business systems analyst.

There are many layers to this publication, and there is no unique author. This book is the equivalent of being able to sit one-on-one and pick the brains of dozens of senior industry professionals and hiring managers and pack that knowledge into easily absorbed content. Don't read this book only once. Leave it on your computer and re-read it from time to time, especially before you put yourself out there in the job market (this includes seeking internal promotions and transfers, as well as applying to new companies). Even hiring managers can benefit from this book if they want to standardize or fine tune their hiring process and maintain question banks for their teams.

Kuebiko Global (www.kuebikoglobal.com) offers a variety of online training and interview preparation packages. Having been in this business for several years, we know that the interview process can be a very intimidating experience for job seekers. Often the students are disadvantaged, as there are not many resources out there that provide a practical, concise approach to learning how to interview successfully. As a result, many job seekers resort either to creating their own study materials from disjointed websites or take a best guess based on their academic training. However, the real world is an entirely different beast than what textbooks present. This information gap provided the impetus for Kuebiko to compile a practical handbook of actual interview questions that will give job seekers the tools they need to succeed.

As professional trainers, we have access to hiring managers who are conducting business systems analyst interviews on a daily basis and constantly improvising their approach to gauging candidates' knowledge in the shortest amount of time. Our trainers also work as industry professionals and cumulatively have conducted hundreds of such interviews. This book reflects these everyday interview experiences, so it's as real as it gets.

That being said, we also want to be transparent. We make no claims to have covered every possible interview question in this book. That would be impossible. Interviewers have their own approaches to conducting interviews; hence, a given question may be asked multiple ways by different interviewers. The intent of the questions and answers presented here is to serve as a broad superset of guidelines for what to expect in an interview. Additionally, each candidate should customize these answers to suit the projects described on their respective résumés, and not merely regurgitate the exact words written here. Each interview is about gauging how compatible your skill set is with the requirements of the job.

To this end, the interviewer will probe your past experience and will attempt to link it to the skill set required for the job. Before stepping into any interview, you should understand the requirements of the position thoroughly, and should customize the answers found in this book to project yourself as the best fit for the job. Always breathe life into the interview by elaborating on your responses with specific examples from your résumé and work experience.

In addition to traditional questions, an interviewer may pose hypothetical scenarios (e.g., mock requirements elicitation) and ask you to present material, draw a process model for a given assignment, or provide a high-level view of your past projects. Those are things that cannot be covered in a book.

Remember, an average interviewer rarely has more than one hour to speak with each candidate. All hiring decisions, either based on the actual answers or the manager's heuristics, are made early on, or within one hour at the most. That is why we have kept this book simple and minimalistic. It's like a real interview where you have around 2-3 minutes to speak at any given time. There might be a lot more information you could present in response to a question, but your speaking time is typically restricted to 3 minutes. Furthermore, interviews proceed with an assumption that your résumé accurately reflects your experience. You are not asked basic subject knowledge questions in an interview, and it usually starts from direct references to your past projects. Hence, this book is not a reference manual where we present flow charts and diagrams to break down and explain the subject of the question.

The aim here is strictly interview preparation, and the assumption is that the reader has already trained or worked as a business systems analyst and has access to some form of study material. Thus, we have made the answers as realistic as possible and have not provided extraneous subject-matter training material.

After going through these questions and answers, you can test yourself by having a friend ask you a few at random, or you can take advantage of our interview simulation package where one of our trainers can simulate a real interview for you and provide recordings. Whatever route you decide to take, ensure that the answers to the questions listed here are internalized and not merely memorized.

Thanks, and good luck with landing the job that you so deserve. We are here to help you at every step, so please feel free to drop us an email with any questions at info@kuebikoglobal.com.

Best wishes,
The Kuebiko Global team

1. Fundamentals of Interviewing

1.1 The Interview Process

Before we get into specific interview questions and answers for a business systems analyst position, let us delve briefly into the fundamentals of a typical interview process. The assumption is that you understand the hiring process and already have a good résumé in place. For additional information, you can log on to our website (www.kuebikoglobal.com) where you will find a webinar on hiring and interview processes, as well as downloadable résumé packs. Let's cut to the chase and assume you have already created a good résumé and are actively seeking on job sites and career portals.

If your résumé is shortlisted, then the first round is usually a telephone screening with the recruiter. The focus at this stage is high-level communication and evaluating how well you can articulate your key skills. It's essential to do well in the initial screening, as recruiters have the power to present you to the hiring manager

The next round is usually a 30-minute to 1-hour telephone conversation with the hiring manager and sometimes his/her colleagues. It is becoming more common now to use video conferencing software, as everyone likes to put a face to a name.

In person interviews, typically last up to a full day and involve meeting with several people. Be prepared to get repetitive questions, as not all companies are efficient, and different people may ask you the same types of questions.

Each interviewer will always start with an introduction to break the ice and will ask you to give an overview of your career trajectory.

Next, you will explain your role and the specifics of your latest projects. You will typically focus on your 2-3 most recent projects.

After this, the interviewer will delve into practical questions, asking how you would deal with specific scenarios. This part might involve some whiteboarding, and you may be asked for your opinion on different approaches in the project lifecycle.

Finally, they will close by evaluating your ethics, your career aspirations, and your level of interest in the job offered. The final question is typically, "Do you have any questions for me?" This is your chance to really get to know the job profile and the expectations. Ask intelligent questions here. This is your opportunity to both showcase your interest in the position and gather more information so you know exactly what you are getting into.

The picture on the following provides a visual representation of what to expect after the first round with the recruiter and a second phone round with the hiring manager.

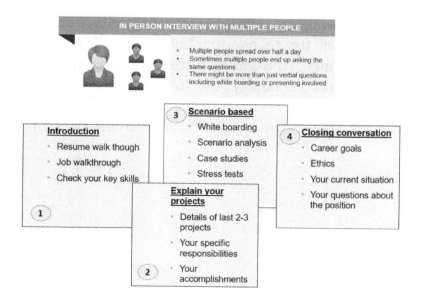

1.2 Common Concerns of Candidates

The following are some common concerns people have about interviews for techno-functional roles like business systems assurance, business systems analysis, project management, and technology recruitment:

Will they ask me random questions on business domain?

No one asks too many questions on technical or domain knowledge besides what you have claimed on your résumé. Business domain and technology are very broad topics, and your interviewer might not know a lot beyond their own area of work. However, certain jobs require expertise in a specific business area. For example, there are many jobs where employers will explicitly point out they need someone experienced in investment banking, telecommunications billing, trade cycles, or a specific regulation in healthcare or financial services. In such job descriptions, the company will identify prior experience in that specific business process that is necessary for the job. So if your résumé explicitly states that you have the requested experience, you may be asked detailed questions about it.

Will they ask me random questions about the dozens of software tools?

Unlike for programmers, tools are a means to an end for business systems analysts and project managers. It's not the end itself. There are far too many tools in the market, and all of them are user-friendly with short learning curves. Thus requirement management or project management software tools will never be the focus of the interview.

Will there be long, vague, certification-style questions?

No. The objective of a job interview is to find out whether you are a good fit for the job being offered. This is very different from obtaining an academic or professional certification.

Will they ask me to name my team members or provide the address of my office?

No, there will not be trick questions used to determine whether you are misrepresenting yourself. The interviewer implicitly trusts you. However, before final offer, background checks are done by third party companies (not by the interviewer or the company itself) to check for red flags or criminal records.

Interviews are meant to evaluate whether you are a good fit for the team and can do the job. They are not like a college exam where all the material covered in your giant textbook is fair game. So prepare efficiently. Do not try to cram in everything at the last minute. Understand the job requirements thoroughly, and carefully prepare based upon the skills and requirements listed in the job description.

2. General Introductory Questions

1) Why did you choose business systems analysis as a profession?

Answer: I have always had a keen interest in the techno-functional domain and being the bridge between technology and business. This is a profession where I can utilize my business domain expertise and interest in technology. Being a people's person, I have the necessary qualities like ability to listen, leadership, facilitation skills and interviewing skills. To sum it up it's a job that is interesting and challenging at the same time and my skills can be best utilized in this field.

2) Describe your latest project and your role in it.

Answer: *This answer is just an example. You will have to describe the latest project on your résumé with the specifics of business value: who uses the system, how many users, its main features, and your specific role. You should be able to give this snapshot in 3-4 minutes.*

The following is strictly an example taken from a student's explanation of a project on his *résumé*. You need to prepare something similar for at least the latest two projects on your *résumé*. In an in-person interview, expect the interviewer to ask you to draw something on the board, such as high level architecture, etc., for the latest project.

Problem: Fannie Mae was handling and restructuring millions of dollars' worth of loans each minute, but the systems they were using were homemade Excel reporting tools. This was initially managed by a huge team of loan processing analysts who used to manually update every single loan detail and restructure them which resulted in inefficiencies mainly slow processing time, which was the result of the loan processing team updating and restructuring loans, periodic reporting since the team reported every month end and inaccuracies due to manual reporting.

Business need: The leadership wanted us to build an OBIEE system that would:

1. Automate the delinquent loan restructuring process to reduce foreclosures and align it with regulatory standards like HUD Hamp guidelines.

2. Report key mortgage metrics on a constant daily basis like mortgage installments, balance, modified interest rate and term of the loan, and LPI dates.

This system offered significant benefits like automation of millions of mortgage reporting and restructuring data, reducing processing time and improving data accuracy.

Action: I defined the problem, documented the overview of the current system, proposed the overview of the new system, and identified the project stakeholders.

I scheduled daily brainstorming sessions with management and cross-functional teams like the reporting team, restructuring team, and the investors' team, etc., to identify, prioritize, and document requirements to define the scope of the system that was to be built.

Next, I worked with the technology team to explain these requirements clearly and concisely, to ensure the deliverables were executed as planned.

I played a pivotal role in project planning by developing short-term and long-term goals, determining the business activities that must be performed to achieve these goals, and scheduling timelines for the deliverables to be met.

I developed out-of-the-box ideas and solutions for the new system integration, which proved to be valuable to the mortgage team. I worked with the IT team to integrate these ideas in to the OBIEE system. Previously, teams from divisions like CLM, DARTS and HSSN had to perform monthly reconciliation of the loans among them. The new OBIEE system offered automated and continuous reconciliation.

Results We achieved great results. The transition to an Oracle-based system reduced processing time by 50% (10 team members would update the Excel reporting every 24 hours, but after transition the Oracle interface automatically updates reports every 12 hours) and improved accuracy by 60% (Accuracy through Excel reporting was 90% and by transitioning to an Oracle interface, we achieved 96% accuracy. Error rate was 10% and we improved it by 6% that resulted in a 60% improvement in accuracy). The project went live 3 months (9 months to 6 months) before schedule without major glitches.

Challenge: Management needed to put all project investments on hold due to significant budget and resource constraints, even pre-committed projects. We were asked to present the needs and benefits to the exec team to see if any deserved special consideration. I put together a cost savings and benefit analysis on reduced staffing (down from 15 to 3 people) to support the process and improvement in key metrics such as accuracy and timeliness, which improved our efficiency by 60%.

Overall, we committed to management that we could ramp this project ahead of schedule and keep within budget ($2.5 million) while gaining significant cost reductions. This convinced them to keep our project funded.

3) What are some things that excite you about your job?

Answer: There are several tasks I complete every day at work that challenge me and keep me interested. Some of them are:
- Improve products by thinking about them from customers' perspectives.
- Use the product in ways that are rarely possible and push the limit on possible usage scenarios.
- Learn new business domains and different business

applications.

- Learn new features and functions of complex software with a very short learning curve.
- Interact with business users to understand how their minds work and how they typically use products.
- Interact with the technology team and quality analysts to understand the different dimensions to test products.

4) Please give me your opinion on the following statement: "A business systems analyst is as good or as bad as his/her domain knowledge."

<u>Answer</u>: I partially agree with it. It depends on the exact requirement of the particular project and the learning ability of the individual. Understanding the industry vertical and processes of that domain in general is very useful. However, domain nuances can be too plentiful, so it might not make sense to restrict oneself in all situations. Additionally, many aspects of the job require generic analysis skills. As long as a person demonstrates a willingness to learn the domain, it's often a short learning curve. However, some projects are highly aligned to specific areas of a domain, and it's better to hire someone who has worked in that area before. I am very familiar with ABC (quote your domain) but am willing to learn new subjects with a very short learning curve if given a chance.

However make sure you know the requirement of that project when answering this one. Sometimes projects require very specific domain knowledge and its best not to apply if you don't have it. If you do have the project domain knowledge of the project you are applying for, you should stress it and claim it as your advantage.

5) If you were hiring a business systems analyst, which traits would be most important to you in a candidate?

Answer: I believe the primary traits a business systems analyst must have are as follows:

- Good analytical skills
- Good communication and leadership skills (facilitative, note taking, documenting, presenting, questioning, and negotiating)
- Engaging, inquisitive, and professional attitude
- Domain knowledge if required

Additionally, I would look for essentials like the ability to articulate their own project domain knowledge in a succinct fashion, awareness of technology architecture, and evidence of involvement in all stages of the software development life cycle [SDLC. However, I'd try to use real life situations and see how they react. For example, I might give them a description of a process and ask them to draw a process flow diagram, put them in mock requirements elicitation session, or ask them scenario-based questions, etc.

6)   If I asked your previous manager what makes you a good business analyst, what would (s)he say?

<u>Answer</u>:
- Great communication and team skills
- Excellent ability to understand the business problem and suggest the most creative, optimum technology solution for it
- Excellent grasp of the big picture
- Very well versed with BA activities at every step of the SDLC
- Out-of-the-box thinker
  - Perfectionistic and passionate about learning

7) If you were to change a few things about how your previous project functioned, what would they be?

<u>Answer</u>:

You need to be careful if asked this one. You should not be too negative about a past employer or manager. Even if you want to point out some flaws, keep it very polite and make sure some positives are also mentioned. The projection should be that those are not flaws but only opportunities for improvement

Some examples include:

I liked my previous (or present assignment) and have been lucky to have a great manager and team. Like any aspect in life, there are some opportunities to improve. For example, when I joined, no one managed the toll gates for documentation limits for each phase of the project, and no one provided templates. Each team had its own set of rules which made it inconsistent from a senior management perspective. I recommended we have a central body with representatives from various teams to control this, and it's in the early stages of formation now.

Another example is that production support on BAU (business as usual) projects was ad hoc, and users would contact the developers directly via a common mail id. I recommended some automation so that we have better reporting, and audit and processing of production-support items. We have recently implemented my suggestion and over time will have a better understanding of the fundamental issues that cause the support tickets and will make more intelligent enhancements.

Other examples include:

- Using very archaic technology and not selling the benefits of newer technology sufficiently
- Project managers should have more domain knowledge
- Building a reusable test suite
- Not having enough touch points where various people working in silos connect with each other

8) Describe your typical day at work.

9) <u>Answer:</u> It's a mix of things depending on what phase of the project we are talking about. In the initial part, it was mostly interacting heavily with the different business user groups like ABC team, XYZ team and PQR team (use team names from your *résumé* projects here) to finalize the scope and detailed business requirements. Then it was liaising extensively with technology leadership to ensure that requirements are communicated and understood. Finally, in the past year, it has been a mix of release planning for sprint cycles, elaborating user stories requires, coordinating UAT, and maintaining product backlog and knowledge documents.

10) In order to achieve the above, I interact with key SMEs (subject matter experts) from the ABC team, XYZ team and PQR team (use team names from your *résumé* projects here). The user base is in the hundreds (or whatever your number is) and so a few key SMEs had been selected by management as the technology liaisons for this project from the business side. They are my user group. I also interact on a daily basis with the technology leads and the development team as required.

11) Where do you see your career going in the short term (3-5 years) and the long term (7+ years)?

<u>Answer</u>: *The answer to this really depends on your interests and the stage of career you are in at this point in time. Use the following career path as a guideline:*

Experience level 0-6 years:

Junior to Mid-level BA with tasks mainly around documentation, assisting senior BA, BA testing with limited client interaction.

Experience level 6-12 years:

Mid to Senior BA. This involves driving requirements management effort, interfacing with very senior level clients, ownership of deliverables quality, and overseeing junior BAs.

Experience level 12+ years:

You can take many routes, depending on your professional aspirations and capability. For example - managing a practice of BAs or combining a senior project management or development management role or being a senior BA with very strong functional expertise in a particular field, etc.

1) Are you a team player or a lone wolf?

2) Answer: I have been in both situations. While I feel teamwork is really necessary to boost morale, enthusiasm, and productivity, I am also comfortable working by myself. From my experience, things like brainstorming, testing strategy discussion, going over user stories and scenarios, and plugging gaps in user stories or user case lists need a lot of teamwork. However, there are things like documentation, preparing presentations, crunching numbers, and data analysis which are best done alone and at the start of the project.

3) Do you like working in small teams or big teams?

Answer: I have had a chance to work in teams as big as 40 people and also in small teams of 3 to 4. While each situation has its pros and cons, I feel comfortable and work well either way.

For example, with a big team, you have more resources and a better division of labor. However, the coordination is challenging and chaotic.

Similarly, small teams can be nimble and are suitable for agile style development. However, the scope has to be limited because of team size, and often the staff is stretched thin and must work longer hours.

4) Have you worked under pressure?

Answer: I am no stranger to working under pressure, and I tend to perform well even under serious time and resource constraints. Even when situations are dire, I am careful not to react impulsively or emotionally and to remain professional at all times.

However, if I notice that the constraints might harm the team or the project, then I prefer talking with my manager about providing additional help in terms of time or resources. For example, in my recent project, there was a situation that resulted from a tight timeline. The entire BA effort for the release of a very visible and significant application was expected to be conducted in just 2 months.

This put a lot of pressure on the entire team, including myself. We had to put in long hours and come in on weekends. The test strategy had to be extremely efficient to make sure that the entire gamut of user stories was tested in that time frame. I ensured that there was a lot of thought put into the plan before we actually started executing the cases. Ultimately, in spite of all the challenges, we delivered the results and ensured that the testing was done in the stipulated time period.

12) Why should we hire you?

Answer: I know that with my diversified experience and knowledge of the business systems analysis process, I would contribute immensely to the success of the project. I am also extremely interested in this kind of role, which is an exact match for my skills and experience.

This is the generic message you want to convey, but in order to establish a perfect synergy and fit, you need to highly customize your answer using items on your résumé that correspond with the skills they are seeking.

13) Why are you looking for a change now?

Answer: There can be many answers to this question based on your personal situation. The objective is to give a perception that the reason you are looking for a change is more than just a paycheck. Also, try to connect it with the key skills required by the job being offered. Never, ever say you are looking for a change because of negative aspects of your current employer (e.g., low pay, bad manager, less work, or bad culture).

Even if one or more of these things truly are the motivation, you should never mention this in an interview. We have provided answers for the most common scenarios below. We have left the skill part generic in the answer, but make sure that you put the specific skill that the employer is looking for in the actual answer that you provide in the interview.

If you are a consultant:

We are at a stage where the project is in a steady state. We've returned more to a 'business as usual' operation with minimal new builds. I am in a contract position, and the need for a full-time BA is likely to end soon. This is why I am looking for a new project where I can add value to the organization while growing professionally. Your position instantly caught my eye because you are looking for someone who is well-versed in <<whatever your key skills are>>. I have been honing this skill for quite some time, and I think there is a great synergy here. My skills could really add value to your project.

If you are in a full-time job:

I have worked at my present employer for X number of years, and it has been a great journey. I still love my job and am very good at it. However, I have hit a ceiling in terms of development there, and I am looking for an opportunity to face new challenges, achieve certain key career aspirations, and grow within the industry. When I read your job description, it immediately piqued my interest as it seems like a perfect match for my skills, and a great opportunity to add value to your organization.

14)   What are you seeking in an ideal job, and why have you chosen our company?

Answer: *You need to do some research on the position and the company in order to answer this question accurately. Add the highlights of the job offered as something you were seeking in a job so that it appears to be a good fit. For example, if the domain is financial services and they want skills in Axure, you can always say that you were interested in adding value using your Axure skills, which is why this job immediately caught your interest. You will need to create the perception of a perfect alignment between your aspirations, job requirements, and the company.*

Here are a few generic characteristics of an ideal job you can state in addition to the customized answer:

- Good work environment

- Work-life balance

- Open communication between management and employees

- Employee-friendly HR policies

- Growth opportunities

15)   What are your strengths and weaknesses as a BA?

Answer: *You need to be very careful with this question. Never, ever state any of the job requirements as a personal weakness. The weaknesses should be very vague and masked as potential strengths.*

For example, "Sometimes I go overboard when given a challenging assignment and work so diligently that my work-life balance suffers." Or, if the position is clearly an individual contributor role, you can always claim your weakness is, "I think I could improve on people management skills, but I'm sure with the right exposure I can be very good at it." Some examples are provided below, but you will need to customize everything for yourself.

Strengths:
- Great communication and team skills
- Excellent ability to understand the business problem and suggest the most creative and optimum technology solution for it
- Excellent idea about the big picture
- Very well versed with BA activities at every step of the SDLC
- Out-of-the-box thinker

Weaknesses:
- I used to take on only one project at a time. However sometimes this can be a detriment if you are hungry to learn and grow and so I have improved my time management abilities and am able to take on multiple tasks and still perform efficiently.

- I have not been a programmer, but I overcame this shortcoming by trying to understand the technology space thoroughly and understand each step in the software development process, from code creation to deployment.
- I used to get impatient when I perceived something as a waste of time. What I feel is redundant might be useful to someone else, and I've learned to take a mature view of things now.

Notice how both the weaknesses are actually masked strengths.

16)   Do you have any questions for me?

Answer: *This is usually the last question of any interview. Make sure you ask a few intelligent questions here. It shows you have the ability to think about the BA process, and it also shows interest in the job. Like many other questions, this is highly specific to the job you are interviewing for. Here are some generic questions you can ask if they have not already been covered during the interview:*

- Will I be working more on technical tasks or managerial tasks?

- Can you tell me more about this project (ask about business gap, which

- department, what stage of development it is in, who are key players, what's the user base, what's the visibility, the technology environment, etc.)

- What are the main challenges you are facing now that I can help with if I join?

- What are some of the key traits you are looking in the new hire?

- What is the success criteria for the job?

3. Big Picture, Enterprise Architecture and Project Initiations

1) Have you been involved with feasibility studies or determined ROI of proposed projects? If yes, what are some ways you determine whether a project is worth executing?

Answer: Answer this in the affirmative, only if you are applying for senior roles as this is not always a part of a BA job. There are many situations that will call for a project, for example, to meet regulatory requirements, to automate manual processes, to effect technology upgrades, or to reduce the cost of operation in the long run.

Out of these, regulatory requirements and technology upgrades are not discretionary. But in the case of a discretionary project, a good deal of cost-benefit analysis must be run.

Some costs and benefits might be qualitative and not quantitative, but one must find out a way to quantify and monetize them. Once you have a logical way of estimating the total cost vs. the total benefit, you can use various ways like showing a positive net present value or a positive return on investment over an agreeable break-even period to prove that the project is worth executing.

2) What are the kind of BA related processes and protocols you would want to set up before starting the project?

Answer: In most projects you join, these protocols will already be established.

However, in rare cases, where there was no BA role before, or if you have to establish a new practice, then you might have to make decisions on the following items:

- Protocol establishment and approaches for requirement gathering
- Protocol establishment and approaches for requirements analysis
- Set artifact expectations to be produced at every step
- Set change management procedure expectations
- Set approval and sign off process expectations
- Performance metrics establishment on which BA responsibilities will be judged

3) What are some of the initial things that you'll do when you start a project?
<u>Answer:</u> There are certain key things that a senior BA should always do after starting a key project that are listed below:

1) **Understand the business case**: It is very important to get the big picture of the project in terms of the business gap it fills, identify its users, the existing set up, high level time lines and the proposed processes and protocols. It is also essential to understand the project's place in the business ecosystem. For example, what is your company's business? What is your department's business? How does the activity of your department contribute to your

company? What is your specific project about, etc.? These items provide a rock solid context to everything you will be doing in the future and ensure that you don't lose sight of the bigger picture when you're involved with the nuances of the project

2) Understand your stakeholders: As a BA, you are as much a relationship manager and the front end for the technology team as you are the functional solution architect. This means a large part of your job is talking to your stakeholders. So it's very mportant to know who your stakeholders are as soon as possible. Stakeholders are not merely users or their representatives. The management, the sign off authority, the representatives of upstream and downstream systems, auditors, and the technology team are all stakeholders. You need to be intimately familiar with all of them and possibly even maintain a RACI matrix to keep track of who's who in the project.

3) Understand the organization structure: This is very important as a BA's role also involves navigating the politics around the project as a part of the life cycle. It involves negotiation, hand holding users when required, managing meetings, and sometimes even selling your solution. For this, it is critical to understand the organization structure and the pecking order.

4) **Understand the existing setup**: Before starting off, one must do everything possible to reduce the learning curve and come up to speed in the project. The first thing I would advise is to understand an existing context diagram, or develop one. This will show you the big picture of the upstream and downstream ecosystem that your application function lives in. Additionally, if it's a project where an old system is being replaced by a new one, then you have the old system as a benchmark. You can get demos, etc., of the existing system and existing documentation to bring yourself up to speed.

5) **High level scope document**: This is the formal beginning of documentation and is sometimes referred to as the high level business requirements document. It establishes the boundary around which the application will be developed. In waterfall projects, it is highly advisable to have this document as the next steps become easier to drill down. Even in Agile development, if some kind of high level scope can be produced in iteration zero, it always helps in setting the context.

6) **Most projects involve working on details of one aspect of a specific functional area where you can easily lose sight of the bigger picture. How do you make sure this does not happen to you?**

Answer: Yes, as a part of being a BA, one does get involved in very granular details; and if one is not careful, it's easy to lose track of the bigger picture when providing a solution. However, I always make sure I ask myself, "How is this adding value to the user, and how is it aligned to the greater mission of the project?" even when looking at minor details. This ensures that I don't lose track of the bigger picture.

To further strengthen your case, give examples from your project where, even while looking at data table level details, you were thinking of how that structure makes it easier for users to access reports; or while figuring out details of UI, you were thinking of making it efficient for end users, etc.

4) What are some of the challenges you have faced in a documenting an end-to-end business architecture and/or a BPM effort?

Answer: Some typical challenges around end-to-end process documentation are:

- **Very few people with holistic knowledge** - For example, my latest project is a workflow engine for a process with 4 major phases. There are people who know their phase very well but do not have an idea about the others. Very few people have a holistic idea about the entire process.

- **Subject Matter Experts (SMEs) do not have time** - Most SMEs I have worked with in the past have been very busy and sought after so getting their time has been a challenge. However, I ensure that I do my homework right in order to make the best use of their time when I am able to schedule time with them.
- **Very little existing documentation** - A lot of projects are created in an ad hoc manner and do not have proper or sufficient documentation.
- **Difference in documentation styles** - Different people have different perspectives and might want things documented differently.
- **Ambiguity** - Standardization is difficult because icons and notations are open to interpretation.

5) What do you think are some ways in which a BA can add value during the development stage?

Answer: Though a chunk of the work during the development stage is for the development team, a BA can add value in the following ways:
- Be available to answer any functional or design question.
- Ensure that the tech design is in sync with the functional architecture.

- Start creating a test plan ahead of time. By doing this, the developer can write code for test cases instead of writing generic code.
- If Agile methodology is being followed then develop user stories, maintain product backlog, and prepare test plans.

6)   Are you familiar with the concept of enterprise architecture? Describe your experience in creating or updating it.

Answer: Enterprise architecture is the process of using visual diagrams and models to describe the big picture of the business architecture and other processes. I have been involved in creating and updating enterprise architecture in many projects. Enterprise Architecture (EA) does not limit itself to any one thing and provides details on various aspects of how the business and corresponding applications run, including business process, operations, data architecture, security, technology infrastructure, etc.
These are very useful for senior management to understand the current state and make decisions on re-architecture or changes to make the entire area more efficient. Some useful artifacts for this purpose are level 1 process flow diagrams, conceptual data models, context diagrams, heat maps of applications within the department, standard operating procedures at high level, and interaction and dependencies charts.

7)   Are you familiar with the concept domain modelling or FACT modeling?

Answer: Yes, I am and have used it in the past.

These are static models that explain the entire business in a very simplistic way. They are also called business entity models. There are depictions of the core business concepts, and then there are logical connections between them called facts. Verbs are used to denote the facts. For example, there might be a concept called 'income' and a concept called 'employee'. A connector connects the two. Relations can be one to one or one to many or many to many, as with data models. The idea is to keep the concepts at a very atomic and granular level so that you understand the details of how the business is structured to the finest level of detail, top down. I have found FACT models to be a very useful source for a start. Using them, we can build very solid data models or business models.

4. Requirements, stakeholder management and SDLC

1)   What are the various life cycle methodologies that you are familiar with?

Answer: I have experience working on SDLC methodologies like Water Fall and Agile primarily (these two are mostly used in the industry, and the ones that you should be most familiar with; especially Agile, since most companies are moving toward it). However, I also know about Spiral Model, Extreme Programming and Rational Unified Process.

In the Water Fall Model, the various phases are sequentially organized. The workable product is not visible until very late in the project. Also, scope change during the project implementation could almost kill the project. This is suitable for projects with usually limited scope.

Agile concentrates on requirements using user stories; simple design, quick releases, daily stand up meetings, pair programming, and no overtime concept.

RUP, which is the industry standard for SDLC, is a configurable software development process platform that delivers proven best practices and a configurable architecture. It is incremental, identifies risks at the early stages, and provides a set of tool mentors including guidelines and templates for successful software development.

2)   Is there any particular methodology you prefer, and why?

Answer: I have no personal preference and am very familiar with both Waterfall and Agile. I have also worked on some projects where there was a company specific SDLC style and a mix of Waterfall and Agile. However, if I were to pick, then it would depend on the type of project.

For fast-paced high-risk projects where the user cannot wait a long time to see the first working prototype, I would recommend Agile. But if one wants to be 100% sure about requirements before starting development, then I would go with Waterfall. Both have their pros and cons, but from my experience, I think an ideal mix based on the specific needs works best.

Expect the discussion to go into pros and cons of each style and your observation after this.

3) What has been your involvement in each of the SDLC stages? Provide detailed examples of involvement in each stage.

Answer: This answer is strictly an example, and you will need to use the project description listed in your resume to come up with an equivalent answer.

When I first joined this project, we were still in the scope and requirements management phase. This was a completely new application we were building to simulate the manual work that was done by the loan analysts. Technology had taken a decision to go for a mix of Waterfall and Agile style development. The requirements phase was managed as per Waterfall but the development was Agile.

For the first three months, my days were mostly spent with the following:

- Studying and analyzing the standard operating procedures and knowledge documentation of the current process
- Shadowing the restructuring team, reporting team, and investment team key SMEs to understand the manual task steps they perform and document it
- Attending recurring in person meetings and making phone calls and sending emails to elicit details of their work

By doing the above, we first produced a scope document that had high level capabilities details required by the business. This built a foundation/fence around which the eventual solution would be built.

For the next month, I was heavily involved in preparation of a detailed business requirements document (BRD), which included nuances of the business requirements, based off the scope document.

Once the detailed BRD was signed off, I created a list of high level user stories based off the BRD. This consumed around one more month.

In this stage, I had a lot of interaction with the technology lead. He provided guidance on the kinds of details he required to ensure sound technology architecture and a smooth iterative development. I would go back to the business teams for any clarification or comments on the requirements. After some back and forth, we arrived at a consensus on the complete list of user stories required in the product.

Subsequently, the development effort started and we had 6 week sprints where I was heavily involved in the following in the past year:

- Release planning on which user stories should go in a particular sprint. I worked with the technology lead to determine this.
- Elaboration of user stories to ensure that the developers had enough detail to successfully complete development.
- Oversight and clarification during the development cycle via scrum sessions.
- Coordinating and managing the UAT and sign off.

- Maintaining a product backlog to ensure that issues would be addressed in future sprints.

4) What are the different elicitation techniques you are familiar with and what are the pros and cons of each of them?

Answer: We have summarized the various elicitation techniques in the table below. You can explain these in words as an answer to the questions.

Elicitation Techniques	People involved	Pros	Cons
User review and feedback on current state document	BA in silo	Refresh user understanding Highlight current gaps, i.e., un-stated requirements	May steer user to focus too much on current state
Provide demo on similar existing applications/ tools	BA with tech	Users have a baseline to provide their requirement Aids in the visualization of requirements	May restrict design of final product by constraining out-of-the-box thinking

Questionnaires	BA to many or one	Can reach bigger user groups Less time consuming	Questions need to be effective and clear Quality dependent on user input and thinking time
Interview	BA with one	Source for in-depth data Relationship building	Time consuming Interviewer prejudice
Observations (day in life sessions)	BA with many	Real behaviour vs. spoken words Generate new ideas	Time consuming Need super users
Use Cases	BA with many	Specific detailed examples providing clarity Guide user thought process	Time investment Risk of not covering non-interactive requirements in use cases
Storyboards	BA with many	Thought provoking Early review of user interface	Possibility of losing the high level objectives because of focussing too

			much on details
Paper/ Interactive Prototype	BA with many	Picture worth a thousand words User involvement at early design stage	Final product may significantly differ from users' expectations
Focus Group/ Workshops (JAD sessions)	BA w1ith many	User buy-in and agreement Discuss subject in depth	Time consuming Getting all the right parties involved at the same time

5) What are some tips for requirements elicitation that you can provide from your experience?

Answer: A few things about requirements elicitation I have learned from my experience as a business systems analyst:

- Put in the effort to really know your stakeholders.
- Establish a plan that supports elicitation success.
- Plan on how to deal with various stakeholder issues.
- Build rapport and respect with stakeholders.

- Be a good facilitator.
- Be creative in using the right combination of elicitation techniques based on the situation.
- Define scope collaboratively and manage it aggressively.
- Be aware of the grey area between requirements analysis and system design.
- Establish and monitor exit criteria so that you know when you are done.
- Lose the ego and shyness - ask questions.

6)   What artifacts have you developed when managing requirements?

Answer: The artifacts I typically create in projects are:

Waterfall:

- Scope document
- Project charter
- High level BRD
- Detailed BRD
- FRD with user stories
- Test plan
- Test cases

Agile:

- Scope document
- High level list of user stories
- Detailed User stories
- Wireframes
- Process flow diagrams
- Basic documents for SIT (System Integration testing) and UAT (User Acceptance Testing)

7) How would you make sure you are not missing any requirements during the requirement gathering process?

Answer: I follow a very organized way, keeping notes and sending MOMs after every relevant elicitation meeting. I also make sure these are documented as soon as possible, because things tend to fade over time. Once the requirements are documented, I make sure I uniquely ID everything and maintain history and versioning. This ensures no information from the elicitation sessions is lost.

8) In your opinion what are the characteristics of a good requirement?

Answer: A good requirement is one that is unambiguous, coherent, cohesive, simple, and cannot be further broken down. Most importantly, it should be testable. For example:

- Tax rate of 10% should be applied on person's income.

- The final risk is a multiplication of severity score and urgency score.
- The total money transferred is a sum of transfer in and transfer out, etc.

9) What was the process you used to prioritize requirements?

Answer: There are several factors that we consider (listed below) that we consider for prioritization before we decide which requirements are high, medium, or low (nice to have) in priority

- Discretionary or compulsory.
- Number of users affected.
- Criticality of occurrence.
- Frequency of occurrence.
- Is there a work around?
- Functional complexity.
- Technical complexity – estimated effort.
- Cost of not doing it.

10) Have you used any requirement management tools? If yes, which ones?

Answer: There are many available in the market but most companies do not use any. Most companies, including Fortune 500 members, depend on MS Office to manage their requirements, and for the most part, even for complex projects, this is sufficient.

Among the tools available, IBM Rational Requisite Pro is commonly used.

Make sure you take a look at the demo and basic features of those tools on their respective websites before you answer this question in the affirmative. It is unlikely the interviewer will ask any detailed questions about the tool, however.

11) How will you react if a technology team member who is very familiar with the system starts thinking about implementation before the requirements elicitation is complete?

Answer: I would politely tell him/her to focus on the business needs during the elicitation, without giving any thought to implementation. Sometimes being prejudiced towards a particular implementation style can jeopardize effective requirements elicitation. It's best to understand the underlying business need before starting to think of how to implement it.

For example, one of the projects I worked on was a tax calculation engine for payroll processing. This system had been in existence a long time, and all the developers were very familiar with the application. This was good for regular production support and operations but bad for the effort to rewrite the entire system. Whenever we were discussing requirements for a system overhaul, the developers knew what to change at the exact field in the tables and the UI panels. They were so married to the system that it was difficult to think out of the box. For example, there was a lot of opportunity to normalize the number of tables used to store tax rates, as it was very inefficient.

The user interface was also much cluttered and could easily be changed to improve navigation. However, the solution design of the future system was getting biased because the technology representatives would immediately look to how the current table or UI could be changed to accommodate the requirement.

Ultimately, we had to explain to them how this approach hampers fresh thought, and we requested they focus only on requirements initially. It worked out pretty well, and we were able to build a new system that was well received by everyone.

12) What are the things that you would put in a BRD against what you would put in a FRS?

Answer: The Business Requirement Document (BRD) is always the business needs without any technical jargon and focuses on "what" is required while the Functional Specification Document (FRD) is a functional solution of "how" to do it.

For example, a BRD will have a one- or two-line description that states the capability needed by the system. It will not provide the solution. The FRD will provide the solution. Some examples of what goes into BRD vs FRD for different types of requirements are provided below:

Process flow: The BRD only contains the level 1 or high level conceptual process flow diagram. The FRD elaborates on this and provides the level 3 which is the operational process flow diagram.

Data requirements: The BRD contains only the data dictionary. The FRD however elaborates on this and has the data flow diagrams, data migration mapping details, and the logical and conceptual data models.

User interface: The BRD contains only the high level requirements of what type of functions are required via the user interface. The FRD, on the other hand, has wireframe details and the specifics of each element involved.

External interface: The BRD will contain only the name of the external interfaces that the system deals with and the context diagram, but the FRD will contain all the details of the data fields that will be exchanged, frequency of exchange, format, etc.

Reporting: The BRD will only contain a basic description of the report. The FRD however will contain all the details like column structure, query criteria, sample data, calculation formula, etc.

13)   You get a feedback saying that your FRD document contained all needed details but was rather long and boring. What would you do to set this right?

Answer: I would consider this as constructive criticism and not get discouraged. I would try to find out specifically what sections could be edited to make it more readable. I would try to portray as much as possible in pictures because people prefer pictures and graphics rather than plain text. I would also try to get it peer reviewed to ensure that it has been validated by multiple people. Additionally, I would also offer a walk through to the approvers to explain the contents of the document if that makes the task of reading through it easier for everyone.

14)   Do you think a BA should be involved in system

design and architecture?

Answer: I think a BA should be involved in the functional architecture and, to a lesser degree, in the actual technical architecture. However, even concerning the technical architecture, it is wise to take inputs from a BA, as required. The BA should understand the underlying technologies that will be used to build the system. At the end of the day, a BA is a bridge between functional and technical teams, and its best that he/she be involved during design to ensure the best solution for the customer.

15)   What are some of the ways of best eliciting requirements if the business users are located in different parts of the globe?

Answer: Phone conversations, video conferencing, screen sharing software, outlook online meetings, etc., are some ways that have worked very well for me.

16)   What are some of the tips for creating good BA documentation?

Answer: For a BA, the most important thing is having subject matter expertise in a project to add value. However, in order to achieve this, the documentation needs to be attractive, accurate, and professional. Some things I have done in the past to achieve this are listed below:

- Have a good logically structured table of contents.
- Have a strong version control in place.
- Write concisely, correctly and consistently.
- Use lots of diagrams, screen shots, examples, and flow diagrams to make your point unambiguous.
- Assume that the audience understands nothing.
- Explain acronyms, abbreviations, and jargon.
- Avoid passive voice, the word 'it', compound sentences, negative viewpoints, and pompous words.
- Have professional and pleasing aesthetics by keeping in mind graphic design principles like white spacing, colour combinations, contrast, and alignment.
- Make it REALLY EASY to read and understand.
- Review several times yourself, and also get it peer reviewed.

17) **Have you used 'use cases' to capture requirements? Was that the only documentation in projects where you did so?**

Answer: Yes, I have absolutely leveraged 'use case methodology' in order to capture requirements. However, I do not recommend using this in isolation. Every documentation style has its limitation, so I would advise using a combination. For example, the BRD style requirements are good for capturing various requirements in isolation but confuse the developers and users about the intended usage or navigation. Whereas use cases are excellent to describe various permutations and combinations of system-user interaction but are not good for capturing details like data models, reporting logic, and non-functional requirements. Hence, in waterfall projects, I would highly recommend having use cases and also a separate business requirements document (BRD).

18) What are the main steps that you'll take in order to write a use case?

Answer: The typical steps I would take for use cases are:

▪ Determine the use case list based on current business needs.

▪ Determine all the actors who would be involved.

▪ Logically package use cases and actors and determine interdependencies.

▪ Start writing each use case, progressively going towards details.

- Graphically represent actor-use case relations using use case diagrams.

- Confirm if all business needs have been captured and if any new ones have been discovered, and go for iterations.

19) Please provide detailed examples of some use cases that you have written.

Answer: *This question should strictly be from the projects on your resume. Do not get into too much detail. Explain around 4-5 of the high level use cases that will be understandable to all. Do not go too deep into your specific project at a level where only you understand. Then explain how you will elaborate by picking one use case. Explain the concepts, like pre-condition, post condition, trigger, steps involved, basic flow, exception flow, and end state. The main contents of a use case are provided below:*

- **'Basic course of events':**

- Provides **main steps of success** in 6-9 steps.

- Actor starts the first step, and system responds till they reach final goal.

- Each step is numbered and is defined as a goal that succeeds.

- **'Alternate paths':**

- These are less common paths that a user can take to achieve the same.

- Every alternate path **starts with the main path.**

- **'Exception paths':**

- These are **for error conditions** and start with basic step.

- 'Extension points': These are the points from where the extensible use cases start

- 'Trigger': Describes 'WHEN' and/or 'WHY' the actor enters the use case.

- **'Assumptions':**

- Place to document items that are assumed to be true.

   - Can also include open items.

   - **'Pre conditions':**

   - These are conditions that must exist even before the start of basic step.

   - Actions in the use case will not check for these.

   - **'Post conditions':**

   - These are the conditions that must be true after the end of the use case.

20)   What do you think are some of the advantages and disadvantages of Use cases?

Answer:

Advantages

- Useful for capturing scenarios where there is system and user interface.
- Gives a very clear picture to developers and users on the exact navigation and usage expected in the system.
- Makes the requirements relatable by bringing the focus on the user rather than the internal mechanics of the system like a FRD does.
- Makes testing traceable and easier.

Disadvantages

- Does not explain various functional modules and their interactions required in the system.
- Does not provide the big picture like the process model or context diagram.
- There is a possibility of missing some scenarios during analysis.
- Not suited for capturing non-interactive requirements like algorithms, mathematical formulae, UI details or non-functional requirements which are better specified

declaratively elsewhere as in the *'Functional Specifications'*.

- Use case theory suggests that UI should not be reflected but excluding that aspect makes **visualization difficult.**
- Not suitable for systems that are better described in a **data/information driven approach** (e.g., data mining system, data reporting, and analysis, etc.). Here the user interaction functionality might be limited but the set of data the system handles may nevertheless be large and rich in details.

21) How do you decide what constitutes a use case and to what level of granularity you must go?

Answer: This is subjective and there are many ways of doing it. I always make sure that I first have a high level listing of use cases based on some categorization in the project. Each individual use case should be one unit of work done by the user interacting with a system. I cross check with all types of requirements (i.e., functional, UI, reporting, non-functional, etc.) to check if I have covered every possible usage scenario.

Once this high level list of use cases is validated by approvers and reviewers in the team, I start expanding each use case and specify the detailed steps. If a particular use case requires mock screens, I provide those too. Typically, I use VISIO for wireframes but am also comfortable with other wife framing tools such as Axure or Balsamiq.

22) What are some checklist items that you would validate before starting walk through for document sign offs?

Answer: Some points I would validate before starting sign off walk-throughs are:

- Is the gap analysis complete and accurate?
- Are all internal cross-references to other requirements correct?
- Are all requirements written at a consistent and appropriate level of detail?
- Do the requirements provide an adequate basis for design and testing?
- Is the implementation priority of each requirement included?
- Does the document include all of the known business needs?
- Is any necessary information missing from a requirement? If so, is it identified?

- Are all non-functional requirements quantifiable and correct?
- Are all requirements uniquely identifiable for future traceability?

23) What are some ways in which changes to requirements can be managed better?

Answer: Change can never be eliminated as many things are not under our control;   however, it can be mitigated by using the following techniques:

- Have a well-planned change management process that is agreed upon and adhered to by all stakeholders at the onset.
- Involve all stakeholders who have the capacity to change requirements involved throughout the requirements management process.
- Encourage participation in all sessions.
- Record all 'Minutes of Meetings' and maintain them.
- Have a solid version control protocol to track changes.
- Notify everyone about changed requirements each time they occur and re-analyze to come up with new time and cost estimates and other impacts.

24) What are some ways in which you can better manage meetings?

Answer: Meetings are an essential part of any techno-functional role and serve many purposes. However, if not managed properly, they can be a complete waste of time and a bottle neck. There are some very specific rules that I have used effectively in the past to manage meetings. They are listed below.

1) Make sure to invite only people required for the meeting. My rule of thumb is that if it's a meeting in which you want to make decisions, then do not invite more than 5 people. If it's a meeting where you need to elicit specific opinion, then invite no more than 15 people; and if it's a monologue meeting where you'll be doing a one-sided talk, like a walk through or a presentation or training, then approximately 50 people is the right size. Anything more than this leads to chaos and inefficiency.

2) Ensure that timing is strictly enforced in all meetings. Otherwise, there is a tendency for the meeting to go on forever, and that is not the most effective use of people's time.

3) Never ever have a meeting without an agenda. Be very clear about the intended outcome and the agenda for discussion before the meeting and provide it in the meeting invitation.

4) Do not come to a meeting unprepared; it wastes other people's time. If there is any preparatory reading you

need to do before the meeting, please make sure you do it.

5) Provide material to attendees far ahead in advance. If you feel there is value in their going through it before the meeting, make sure you request they do so.

6) Enforce rules of how much one can talk, and if someone deviates from the agenda, be polite but forceful about bringing the group back to the concerned topic.

5. BA - User interface design based questions

1)   What are some basic questions you'll consider before starting user interface (UI) design?

Answer: Some questions that I will consider before starting UI design are:

•   What is the profile of your user/users

o Personality type

o Geographic locations

o Age

o Gender

• What is their level of computer knowledge?

• What are the main user cases/user stories they will be solving to use your system?

• What is their current way of managing those user stories?

• What devices and browsers will they be using?

• What screen resolutions and operating systems are they comfortable with?

2) What are some basic questions you'll consider for information display on the screen?

Answer: Some basic questions to consider for information display are:

- Is the user interested in precise information or data relationships?

- How quickly do information values change?

- Is it mostly static information on display or dynamic information?

- How diverse and complex is the source of dynamic information, if applicable?

- Is information textual or visual?

- Are relative values important?

- What are the various actions on the screen and what kind of responses are required by the system in how much time?

3) What are some basic UI design considerations?

Answer: Some basic UI design considerations are as seen on the following page:

User familiarity	The user interface must be drawn from concepts and visual notations and verbiage that the users are familiar with.
Consistency	The interface should be consistent with the functions that are similar so that user learning is easier.
Minimal surprise	Keep actions intuitive and self-explanatory so that the user is not surprised when a system does a particular thing.

Recoverability	If the user makes a mistake for some reason, it should not be irreversible.
User guidance	Use help texts, mouse roll overs, pop-up helps, and logical design based on usage to ensure that the user never feels lost in the system.
User diversity	Understand there can be several different types of users that use your system, and your design should consider lowest common denominators to suit everyone.

4)   You have been provided requirements and explanation for a new application to be built. How will you go about approaching initial UI design?

Answer: I would take the following steps to come up with a first draft of the wireframes:

- The first step is to completely understand the user base, demographic, their preferred style, any previous systems they are used to, level of engagement with the system, etc.

- Next I will identify the main functional groups into which the application is split.

- Then I will identify the main use cases to determine the main ways in which the user will interact with the system.

- These three items will provide enough information to create a main site map and landing page. I cannot stress enough the importance of the landing page to ensure that the rest of the application flows smoothly.

- This is then validated with the main users, and a working prototype is created page by page in a UI tool like Axure.

- There will be several iterations and all logical feedback will be incorporated back into the wireframe.

- The final prototype is signed off by all parties, and the UI is created based on the final prototype.

5)   How do users typically locate information on the User interface (UI)?

Answer: Generally speaking, users scan for information on the UI. The scan is very quick and use only for the information they are really looking for. As they say, if users can't find a product, they can't buy it. Meaning users typically have less time and memory to remember things on the UI. They want to locate information in an easy way. For example, users want to see highlighted text or keywords, meaningful headings and sub-headings, a single idea for a paragraph, etc.

6) How would you plan for UI consistency?

Answer: There are several aspects to UI building and like anything, planning is an essential part of the initial groundwork. Important aspects such as having consistent navigation paths, consistent behavior of buttons/links, etc., are very crucial. It is also extremely important to have consistent fonts and sizes, spacing, and color schemes.

Before getting into any sort of implementation, it helps if the design team or business analysts, or the design team and business stakeholders work on planning the aspects of the UI. Even involving implementation SMEs helps, as they can provide feedback on how to keep UI consistent and give input on feasibility of system components.

7) What are wireframes created for?

Answer: Wireframes are the "initial designs" of the UI. They are also called prototypes. Wireframes are created in the initial development stages for seeking quick feedback on the requirements and general expectations of the business team and SMEs from the solution. They will have necessary and important elements of the user interaction with the application and basic data types and aspects, such as mandatory optional data fields. Usually, wireframes are created using wireframing products available in the market. These also typically support ways to provide online feedback and corrections from the stakeholders. This process speeds up initial buy in of the solution being developed.

8) What are typical contents of a visual design?

Answer: Visual designs are typically extensions to wireframes. Once wireframes are approved, the next development stage of detailing of the visual designs can begin. Typical visual design contents are usable (simulated) screens with navigation support which will be fully in sync with what users will see on the finished UI. It will also include color schemes and fonts/sizing which will resemble the final solution (the actual "app" or back-end is not in place though). Just like wireframes even visual designs are review approved and then are enabled for the development process.

9) Explain one of the key principles of UI design- keep only required elements.

Answer: This is basically the practice of keeping things simple. Users, if bombarded with too much information, too many data elements to fill can easily lose interest. The idea is to keep only essential elements on the UI. Avoid unnecessary elements or data entry parts if they can be deferred or even eliminated. For example, even a simple UI for a website registration can be intimidating if too much mandatory information must be supplied before a user can check basic features of the site, via registration. If it is simplified with just email ID and password, users will be more likely to register, thus generating more interest in the website.

10) What are typical navigational aids used to assist with comprehension and logical understanding?

Answer: Typical navigational aids are icons, demos, search, sliders, and in-line help text. These are simple ways to help the user understand the context and use the given operation and help text. FAQs are also very helpful in designing good UI.

11) What are typical mistakes a user makes on UI?

Answer: Typical user UI mistakes are exiting without saving, incorrect data entry and not providing amendments, forgetting passwords or other such information, initiating a transaction twice or more, etc. Recommended practice in designing a good UI is to avoid these typical user errors by using proper UI design principles.

For example, a user may have entered a good deal of information on the UI already and may exit without saving, or due to connectivity loss, all his or her input data may be reset or lost. To deal with such cases, it is essential to anticipate user errors and provide features such as auto-save and/or a warning message that indicates the user has not saved the data, and ask whether he or she intends to save it.

12) How does working memory of a human being affect user interface design?

Answer: Studies prove that the maximum number of objects a human can hold in his working memory is 7. In other words, more than 7 active elements becomes difficult for the human brain. Without taking it exactly by number, the idea is to use this finding in UI design and make sure there are limited active elements on the UI and preferably just a few at a time on which the user can focus.

13) What will you consider during writing a product specification for an online store? What will you show in preview and what will you show after click through?

Answer: The key is to provide essential information—not too much, not too little. While displaying product specifications, for example, just showing the price and image would be insufficient information, even though further product detail is available by clicking. The additional click is one more user step.

In order to provide greater user ease of operation, it is helpful to provide item information preview, image and price, on first view. For users interested in more information, you can provide a link to details. All these decisions, of course, are subject to stakeholder agreement as well.

14) What are particular considerations you will give for designing UI for mobile web?

Answer: The onset of having web apps as mobile web apps has transformed the way business analysts and designers should be looking at UI aspects. If the app is to be supported on mobile as well, then some of the key considerations are screen real estate, target handset, and deciding what the most important features are to be provided on the mobile app. As mentioned earlier, target handset plays a key role (including its screen area). For example, on an iPad, the available real estate is much greater compared to smaller size smartphones. And for each target, UI rendering could be different.

15) Why is it important to understand how the users operate any of the currently existing systems?

Answer: Let me explain the answer in the context of typical transformation projects. Typically, existing legacy systems are using traditional UI, and the new products being designed are completely state of the art UI and based on fine design principles. In such cases, getting an insight into how existing systems operate may be overlooked.

The analyst and/or designer should be careful to avoid this. A familiarity with the existing legacy system in terms of data entry, operations, errors, integrations, if any, and user feedback helps, as the new product can be designed to not only address current needs but to also improve usability. The goal is to not confuse users in terms of finding the tools they need on the UI. Sometimes adopting similar terms from existing UI can help; and at times, new and creative terms on the UI may ease the operation and provide value.

16) Why is it important to understand the user base while designing UI? Give examples?

Answer: The user base basically means gaining an insight into who the end users are, where they come from, what their profile looks like, their age band, and their preferences to use software or a solution like the one being developed. Do we have any feedback from users of the existing application and many more applicable information in the context of our project?

For example, an online platform such as Amazon has users spread across the globe, originating from various countries. But even in a single country, buying preferences are likely to be unique, and it is important to understand users so that the solution can provide unique value to each of them, thereby increasing sales and revenue.

17)   How important is feedback in user interface design? How will you go about securing it from stakeholders?

Answer: Early feedback on user interface design is very crucial. All business stakeholders, business analysts, implementation SMEs, project managers, and users are in turn sources of feedback for usability or the design team. The more closely and collaboratively the team works, the easier it is to find errors earlier, understand user preferences earlier and sync the product or solution with overall requirements.

18)   As a business systems analyst, you want to link requirements with wireframes. What are possible ways in which you can do this?

Answer: There are several ways. Basically, it is a question of traceability of development artifacts so either they can be linked through a dedicated traceability matrix for each functional requirement (linked to screens related) or even a simplified Agile version of it such as providing a reference to the user story in the screen definition and vice versa. In most of my projects, it is done through implicit linking of requirement artifact with the screen which is or are related. However, various options are available to suit the given project needs.

19) What ways can you make sure you are using users' vocabulary for UI?

Answer: A simple way is to define key business terms in a glossary or data dictionary and publish it on a common project repository. These terms are basically cues to be used while determining the key UI terms and names. Additionally, even existing apps and going over existing documents can also provide information on what other common terms users have used for the UI.

20) Give examples of widgets you have created or used.

Answer: I have used typical widgets such as list box, combo box, radio buttons, links, buttons, menus, tabs, etc. In other projects, I also used widgets such as tree view, status bar, progress bar and tooltips. For a file upload function, for example, it is valuable to see the upload progress using a progress bar.

21) Give examples of how you can prevent errors using UI?

Answer: There are different ways in which UI errors can be prevented. For example, providing default data values will prevent errors related to incomplete or wrong data entry. Additionally, we can provide several alerts and notifications on potentially incorrect or invalid data entry thereby preventing later errors. As an example, end date earlier or same as start date is a validation error which can be prevented during data entry on UI, by providing the user with an appropriate alert.

22) How important is feedback in user interface design? How will you go about securing it from stakeholders?

Answer: Early feedback on user interface design is very crucial. All business stakeholders, business analysts, implementation SMEs, project managers, and users are in turn sources of feedback for usability or the design team. The more closely and collaboratively the team works, the easier it is to find errors earlier, understand user preferences earlier and sync the product or solution with overall requirements.

23)   As a business systems analyst, you want to link requirements with wireframes. What are possible ways in which you can do this?

Answer: There are several ways. Basically, it is a question of traceability of development artifacts so either they can be linked through a dedicated traceability matrix for each functional requirement (linked to screens related) or even a simplified Agile version of it such as providing a reference to the user story in the screen definition and vice versa. In most of my projects, it is done through implicit linking of requirement artifact with the screen which is or are related. However, various options are available to suit the given project needs.

24)   What ways can you make sure you are using users' vocabulary for UI?

Answer: A simple way is to define key business terms in a glossary or data dictionary and publish it on a common project repository. These terms are basically cues to be used while determining the key UI terms and names. Additionally, even existing apps and going over existing documents can also provide information on what other common terms users have used for the UI.

25) Give examples of widgets you have created or used.

Answer: I have used typical widgets such as list box, combo box, radio buttons, links, buttons, menus, tabs, etc. In other projects, I also used widgets such as tree view, status bar, progress bar and tooltips. For a file upload function, for example, it is valuable to see the upload progress using a progress bar.

26) Give examples of how you can prevent errors using UI?

Answer: There are different ways in which UI errors can be prevented. For example, providing default data values will prevent errors related to incomplete or wrong data entry. Additionally, we can provide several alerts and notifications on potentially incorrect or invalid data entry thereby preventing later errors. As an example, end date earlier or same as start date is a validation error which can be prevented during data entry on UI, by providing the user with an appropriate alert.

27)   Can you think of UI considerations for a multilingual ecommerce site?

Answer: Some multilingual considerations are quite common, such as providing a language switch option (which changes UI text as well as even the keypad if necessary), automatically changing the currency based on country/language selected, changing payment gateways internally and similar actions. An easy to locate change country/change language and change currency and all related options must be provided on such an ecommerce site. Many times a full translation process is needed to convert the UI text, rather than just word by word conversion. Expert tools are available for this task.

28)   What considerations would you provide on user interface defaults?

Answer: As mentioned before, some of the UI fields can easily be defaulted, e.g. currency for the country, values such as start date (defaulted to current date), and defaulting selections for some of the list or combo box items. Such defaults eliminate user effort by saving time on obvious data entry tasks.

29) What do you mean by response latency when it comes to user interface design? Where would you capture requirements in this area?

Answer: Latency basically is the time between user action initiation and site/application response. Response time and site performance requirements are captured typically as non-functional requirements and documented as part of the system or functional requirements specification. It helps to check requirements in this area with business stakeholders as well as technical or development teams to ensure the requirements are feasible.

30) What will you consider when writing product specifications for an online store? What will you show in preview and what will you on click through?

Answer: The key is to provide essential information, neither too little nor too much. While displaying product specifications, showing just the price and image provides insufficient information, even though fuller product detail is available on click. But this adds one more user step. It would be helpful to provide item preview, image, and price on the page and provide a link to more details. Of course, any such implementation requires stakeholder agreement as well.

31)   At what stage would you incorporate organizational standards for the user interface?

Answer: Organizational standards are best identified and planned for at the initial stage of the project. It is helpful to find the tools available in the organization for capturing wireframes and visuals. Also having knowledge on UI standards, colors, fonts for the program or project you are working helps too. At any later point during the project also, it is important to track changes, and not newer trends in the organizational UI standards and assess impact if any.

32)   Which tools have you used for building user interface designs?

Answer: I have used Axure, MockFlow, Visio, and Balsamiq to name a few. I have also found most of these tools are fundamentally the same in assisting analysts and designers with creating UI elements, screens, navigation, and screen flows. Each has its pros and cons. For example, Balsamiq supports wireframes that are more of the hand-written kind, whereas MockFlow or Axure supports more formal looking UIs which some stakeholders prefer.

33) **The business users of the current product are too used to the existing system. For the new strategic product these users are not fully comfortable with the concept. What would you do to increase their participation level in user interface design?**

Answer: I would build a rapport with the stakeholders by using the terms and concepts they are familiar with in the existing system. I would also work on creating a better and completely different version of the UI and get buy-in from the stakeholders wherever I would think it is essential to break older ways.

34) **What are your views on testing aspects of user interface design? If you have a separate design team, when would you like to involve them?**

Answer: Testing of UI design per se is somewhat quantitative and qualitative testing. In straight forward or qualitative testing, as BA, I would create tests that would test the function as per original requirements and design. It is still helpful to involve the design team in review of the tests and actual testing.

35) What are typical elements of website wireframes?

Answer: Navigation components such as pagination, search, slider, and tags. Input controls such as checkbox, list box, radio buttons, text field, and date fields. And then there are informative components such as status and progress bar and modal windows.

36) In which project initiatives, as a business analyst, would you consider doing wireframing and visual design yourself and in which projects would you recommend having a separate design team?

Answer: With smaller projects or projects that are not very UI intensive, it is usually sufficient if the business analyst does the wireframing himself or herself. For larger projects and/or projects where intensive UI considerations are helpful and there is dedicated budget for such a team, a separate design team should be put in place. Even if funding is available on the project only for certain phases or a limited duration, project benefits can be very high in such cases.

37) How would you go about relating UI screens with use cases?

Answer: A single use case specification can have main flow and several alternate and exception flows, each of them having a separate UI screen. It is helpful if there is a reference provided in use case specification for the screen related to it.

38) What are typical challenges in wire framing process?

Answer: There are several challenges in wireframing a product as listed below

- A typical challenge is that stakeholders consider the wireframes as final design and not as a prototype to be evaluated. I have faced this in couple of projects and the way to take care of this is to set the right expectations with the stakeholders and encourage feedback.

- The stakeholders do not always knows what they need unless they use the product. So you may end up doing the prototyping several times

- Not all systems can be completely explained by prototypes. For example, if it's a complex trading system or a claims processing system then a simple prototype might not do justice to what the final product will feel like.

- Different users have too many different opinions on how the screens should look feel and flow

- Users might not be able to pin point the exact flaws with the prototype but make very generic comments that they do not like it

39) Would you create separate personas for separate demographics in persona-based UI design?

Answer: Personas are fictional characters that a UI designer uses to think through what would work best for a real user. We always consider very real characteristics such as likes, dislikes, goals, usage patterns, personality types, and demographics.

Demographics thus is a key factor in the way a persona might use a system. For example, the way a female 25-year-old Latina from California uses a particular system can potentially be very different from the way a Caucasian 55-year-old from Texas uses it. So I would say that demographics can surely be a distinguishing factor when deciding personas. However, it is not the only factor. There might be other occasions when the demographic is not so much a differentiator. Hence, whether or not to use demographics causes me to separate personas is totally dependent on the usage and the application in question. It's impossible to create a rule of thumb.

6. BA – Data Modeling Related Questions

1) What are the main types of activities related to data that you have been involved with as a BA?

Answer: I've been involved with the following types of data related activities as a BA in the past:

    a. Creating data flow diagrams

    b. Creating data dictionary

    c. Creating data models

    d. Data mapping between systems

    e. Creating data visualizations

    f. Basic data analysis using SQL

2) How comfortable are you with SQL and data analysis?

Answer: I am comfortable with basic and some intermediate SQL for basic data analysis. During some points in past projects, I have had to use SQL to fetch data for analysis myself. However, for any complex queries I always asked someone from the development team

Note that as a BA you might be expected to do some basic SQL but unless the job requirements specifically state so, you need not be an expert.

3) How much have you been involved with data modeling?

Answer: I have been extensively involved with data mapping, creating data dictionary and data modeling exercises. However, in data modeling, it was more a conceptual and logical data model. The development team managed the physical data model.

I always first try and look at the big picture and broad categories of requirements that will have an underlying data need in the system. These will become elements of my conceptual data model. At this stage, we avoid all details like primary and foreign key and focus only on the high level functional structure of how the database should be optimally architected. Once we have a final conceptual data model, I start adding details to each entity and mark the relationships between them and specify keys. I try to keep it optimal, so it's easy to create the physical data model based on my conceptual model, there are no redundancies, and system performance is optimal.

4) In a data model, can you give some examples of entity and related attributes in a real life scenario?

Answer: We can consider simple real life project situations such as an online banking system wherein customer and account are the business entities. Each entity has attributes that describe more information about it, for each customer has attributes such as first name, last name, address fields including zip code, contact number, account number, etc. Each account is another entity and its related information is account type, account unique id, and account balance.

5) For an attribute of zip code, what would be typical

values associated with it?

Answer: Zip code can potentially contain the following values - country (country where the address is originating from), format (country-specific zip code format) and actual code value. Each will also possess the type of the value fields such as alphabets or alphanumeric.

6) Tell us something about entity associations and cardinalities.

Answer: In the real world, entities are often associated with each other and are never standalone. The way in which entities get linked to each other during modeling are called associations. For example, a computer is assembled using several parts such as CPU, screen, speaker, mouse, and keypad. Each computer is associated with these components in a one-to-one manner (generally speaking) and in such cases the association is identified as one-to-one (1-1) at both ends of the link (computer to CPU, computer to keyboard, etc). Type of association is labelled as cardinality, and it can range from 0 to n on each side. Typical cardinalities are 0-n, 1-n, 1-1, m-n.

7) For a typical shipment tracking process, can you come up with an essential entity relationship diagram?

Answer: A shipment tracking system is typically comprised of ongoing shipment status at every point in time during its journey from source to destination. Typically, the important shipment statuses are called milestones. The essential entity relationship diagram will contain one entity for shipment notice and another for item and milestone. Shipment and milestone are associated with each other in a one-to-many relation. Shipment and item are also associated with each other in a one-to-many relation. Shipment will have attributes such as shipment ID, customer name, customer number, and customer shipping address. Item will have attributes such as product ID, product name, quantity, price, and unit of measure. Milestone will have attributes such as current location address, city, country, zip code, and time to reach destination.

8) A project is using some additional information about legal data being used, such as when and why the data was created, when it was changed, etc. What is this kind of data called?

Answer: Such data is called regulatory and historic data and is one of the important data to be maintained as part of an organization's information repository. For example, for a tax consulting firm, all the data about tax payers is legal data, and it needs to be maintained in some countries, by law, for at least 7 years.

9) What is the difference between primitive and composite data while creating a data dictionary? Can you give some examples of it in the context of

subscriber information for a typical ecommerce sites?

Answer: Primitive data is data that cannot be subdivided further, in other words, atomic information. Composite data is comprised of primitive fields. For example, subscriber data will have first name and last name as primitive attributes, whereas address is usually a composite field that includes (address field1, address field 2, city, state, country, and zip code) each of the fields within it being a primitive field individually.

10) While building a data dictionary for a purchasing system, you are building from scratch, which stakeholders are you likely to have involved and how would you go about preparing it?

Answer: For building such a data dictionary, I will typically involve the domain SMEs and implementation SMEs. I would initially look into existing documentation about the project and ask my manager or point of contact for the right people to contact to build this, suggesting they should be from domain groups and the implementation team, plus any additional contacts he may help identify. Based on existing documentation or knowledge about the project, I would build part of it myself first and then go about planning for a review/refinement of it with the identified stakeholders.

11) What do you think are limitations of a data dictionary?

Answer: Main limitations are that it is unfamiliar and hence may be unacceptable to certain non-technical users; secondly, it does not describe any of the functional detail. The second point is not really a limitation but something one should be aware of.

12) Do business rules represent a data model? In what ways?

Answer: Yes business rules also are components of the data model. For example, tax slabs typically have salary range and applicable tax in the form of a table. In turn, it describes the relation between salary, tax, and allowable values. Hence it is a form of a data model itself and can be built at the conceptual as well as logical level.

13) The data structure you have created for your project is potentially reusable across several other initiatives across the organization. How would you go about standardizing the same?

Answer: Once determined that it is likely be reusable, I will ask the project point of contact, such as the project manager or the BA line manager, for similar data definitions across all known projects. I will also figure if there is any organization standard location on wiki or SharePoint where we already maintain such reusable artifacts. If not, I would suggest the team create one and talk through the standardization activity I am working on with project stakeholders and get their buy-in. Once done, I will also ask for feedback across the teams to make sure we have common definitions of the program or organization level data.

14) What is the difference between glossary and data dictionary?

Answer: Glossary contains key project terms, their aliases and descriptions and serves as the single source of all such terms. It does not have a formal structure or format though. It is more for business users and domain subject matter experts (SMEs) in that sense. A data dictionary is a more technical repository which, like a glossary, also is used to have consistent definitions across the board, remove redundancy, etc. A data dictionary is a key step in creating databases and has information such as name, data type, constraint, etc., about each data, hence it is a technical artifact.

15) The project you are working on involves a great deal of data around pick request, pack request, commercial invoice, shipment notice, etc. All of it is interrelated. The stakeholders with domain knowledge are not really comfortable with ER diagram and technical terms. What options would you consider for representing given data correctly and in an easy-to-read manner?

Answer: I will, in such cases, create a business or conceptual diagram with essential attributes only defined during stakeholder reviews. I will also consider accompanying the same with a mind-map diagram to describe central concepts and linked objects and their fields. It is quite easy to grasp a diagram such as this, especially for complex concepts such as ones stated in the question.

16) What is the difference between conceptual data model and logical data model?

Answer: Conceptual data model is at a business level and is used to clarify the entities in scope and their overall relations to each other. It may not have all attributes defined and types of data and any other granular information about data. Once the conceptual data model is agreed upon with stakeholders, business analysts typically move on to develop it further with the logical data model which has extensive information about each entity such as data type, all relations defined precisely, constraints, etc.

For example, a conceptual data model for a banking system may have entities such as customer, account, and transaction; and it may have very limited information about each entity. For example, customer will have only first name, last name, SSN number, and address. Entities may have only preliminary relationships jotted down. However, in a logical data model, each of these entities will have complete details such as all attributes about each entity, their types of constraints, etc., plus a precise and complete set of entity relationships.

17) Explain how you would typically go about analyzing entity relationships.

Answer: Many types of initial project documentation, such as project scope document, business case, and business requirements specifications are great sources for finding the key business entities involved. For example, terms such as subscriber, message, links, and segments, if mentioned in the SOW (statement of work) document are an indication that they are indeed the key business terms. Once these are identified, I would initially draw upon understood relations or cardinalities purely by common sense knowledge. I will note open questions clarifications on each and then take it for review with identified stakeholders for further refinement.

18) What are the benefits of using a data warehouse? Do you have project experience in it?

Answer: A data warehouse contains non-transactional and historical information about company and project data and is used typically for uncovering specific patterns and any other analytical information about the data for reporting purposes. I have not directly worked on DW projects; however, most of my projects involved data which was in turn used by several data warehousing projects across the organization. So I am aware of key concepts around it.

19) What is the level of information detail a conceptual

data model can have?

Answer: As discussed previously, information detail at data model level is likely to be the basic or minimal amount required to understand key attributes of each entity. For example, the conceptual model may contain subscriber information at essential level such as name, address, contact details, date of birth, and gender. It may not have full-fledged information about address fields, and it may not have custom data yet.

20)You, as a business analyst, are in the process of eliciting business requirements and need to create a conceptual data model for the project. How would you go about eliciting this information?

Answer: For elicitation activity, be it of any kind, either data such as conceptual model or process such as process flow, I follow a standard process which concentrates a lot on preparation such as identifying stakeholders, setting up meetings, preparing and going over existing resources and creating a questionnaire on the topic. In the actual meeting, I go over each of the models created, field questions and then seek online feedback from SMEs. Ideally, if we have enough time, changes should be done immediately to reduce offline work and rounds of review. Once done, I send out the updated documents and models to each participant and ask for confirmation of the results so that it is approved and can be taken to the next stage.

21) **What would a conceptual model for an online shopping platform look like?**

Answer: Typical business entities are buyer, product, order, invoice, and shipment. I can draw it on paper for you but general cardinalities would look like this: order to product (1-n), buyer to order (0-n), order to invoice (1-n), and invoice to shipment (1:1).

22) **Which of the models are DBMS platform/technology independent?**

Answer: Conceptual and logical models are technology independent whereas physical data models are technology dependent and are closely dependent on database management system (DBMS) platform selection.

23) What do you think are the key issues or aspects to be considered during data modeling?

Answer: Common mistakes I have seen involve having overly large data models rather than simplified entities, insufficient reviews from domain SMEs as well as implementation SMEs, and not keeping the models up-to-date.

24) Tell us about Unified Modelling Language (UML) class model with very specific examples from your projects?

Answer: UML has its own structure for creating a class model, and I have worked on creating one in one of my earlier projects. Class model is used at the logical modeling stage. Class model should contain data type, constraints if any and cardinalities defined at a detail level. I had used the class model for an employee onboarding project I was working on and had used the tool Rational Rose for the job. To be specific, I had created the class model using entities such as employee, department, project, and joining formality and each had attributes detailed using this tool. The tool also enforced the relationship (0..1, 0..n etc) cardinalities stated diagrammatically.

25) What tools have you used for data modelling?

Answer: I have used Rational Rose in earlier projects. In most of my later projects, I have used Visio when the organization has that as its standard. For some clients, I have used cloud based and online free tools such as Lucidchart for the same purpose. Erwin is also a market leader but it's more involved and suited for database professionals.

26) Tell us something about generalization with very specific examples from your projects?

Answer:
Generalization is a recommended practice per UML and is quite helpful in data modeling as I have experienced in my projects. I was working on creating a conceptual data model for all types of users involved in the system. The users were UK and US users.

Further analysis and generalization reveled each group had its individual characteristics. I ended up creating a general user called online user and all country specific users got linked in an abstraction with this user.

27) What are the rules or constraints that are useful in designing a logical model?

Answer: Typical constraints or rules are, for example, date can only be in MM/DD/YYYY format. Another can be zip code being strictly 5 digits.

28) What are typical mistakes in analyzing conceptual data model? How they can be prevented? Give me examples from your projects.

Answer: Typical mistakes as discussed before are insufficient reviews, not keeping models up to date, and large data models. Mistakes like this can be prevented using good requirements practices, such as clear entities and terms, review feedback mechanism for refining the models, appropriate level of participation from the stakeholders, facilitated approvals, and good analysis that leads to a "normalized" and simple view of the business entities involved.

29) How would you go about managing the changes to conceptual and logical data models?

Answer: Like any requirements artifacts, I would make sure that a review/approve and change management process is set and being followed for the given project. On-time reviews and approvals and accurate record-keeping on exact changes help a great deal in the long run.

30) What stakeholders would you typically involve for creating a conceptual data model? Give me examples from your projects.

Answer: For creating a conceptual model for online retail store I was working on, I involved all the domain SMEs and project managers and some of the end users as well. Key reviews were with domain SMEs, which were globally located, hence the review rework was collaborative and online.

31) What stakeholders would you typically involve for creating a logical data model?

Answer: For a logical model, I would closely involve the database architect, team leads, and other dev SMEs so they are also able to participate in creating a logical model in a collaborative way. Particularly rules, constraints, data types, org standards, and confirmation on cardinality are the areas I would watch out for.

32) Give me examples of when you have used top down

approach and when you have used bottom up from your projects?

Answer: Most of my projects involved data modelling done in a top-down manner, i.e., starting from requirements to detailed models. In some cases, such as reverse engineering projects or when there was no requirements and models existing but databases were in place, I had to follow a bottom-up approach.

33) All in all, what is the sequence of things that a BA does with the data portion of the project?

Answer: The BA does the following items with data in the project:
- BA is the person that **first gathers the data requirements** of a system as explained in the BRD and FRD.

- Data requirements are explained in a very granular manner in the **data dictionary, data mapping, and data models.**

- The **BA also collects the reporting requirements**, which are basically how the users should or want to consume the underlying data in the system.

- The reporting combined with the data dictionary and data model provide information on **what form of data visualization** is best suited for the scenarios.

- Based on the choice of data visualizations, the BA also provides most **templates of how various reports, views, and dashboards** will look like in the system.

- Using the data dictionary, data model, and data visualization mock screens provided by a BA, the development team executes and builds a working system.

7. Business Process Modeling and UML

1)   What are the high levels steps you would take if asked to do process modelling for a project?

<u>Answer:</u> **The steps I would take to model business processes for an area are:**

Scope determination - The first step would be to determine the scope of the effort. Businesses are often intermingled, and the scope can potentially be limitless. It is therefore essential to be clear about what part of the process we are going to model in this particular endeavor.

Absorb existing information – After scope is determined, I would gather all the information that is available about a particular area. This would include reading any existing documentation, understanding the players involved, understanding the business purpose, and if any system exists which is being actively used. This is like my homework so I can make the best use of people's time when I get to the next step of interviewing them.

Interviewing the stakeholders – I would then go and speak in detail with the people who are a part of the existing process. If the documentation does not already exist, I would document the current process in detail. This usually sets the pace for the future state documentation and also makes me intimately familiar with the subject matter. I go step by step trying to understanding the business nuances, dependencies, reasons, rules and risk behind every step. To put together a visual flowchart, I either use BPMN, if that's the standard of the organization, or simple VISIO with basic iconography if users prefer it that way.

Confirm and fine tune – The final step is to share my first draft with all the key stakeholders and check to see if everyone is in agreement with the representation. There is usually back and forth at this stage, and people might ask for updates. We make as many iterations as required and arrive at the final draft.

2) What does BPMN stand for? What is the difference between BPMN, BPM and BPMS?

Answer: BPMN stands for Business Process Modeling Notation. It is an industry standard for process modeling. BPM is a methodology and framework for process design and improvement. It is based on DMAIC – Define, Measure, Analyze, Improve, and Control - six sigma principles. BPMS stands for Business Process Management Software and is a suite of applications that support process design, automation, improvement and monitoring- such as Appian Suite, PEGA, etc. Many times these terms are used interchangeably though.

3) Are you familiar with BPMN? How much have you used? What are some challenges you have observed with it?

Answer: Yes, I am familiar with the fundamentals of BPMN and have used the basic notations. I have a BPMN-enabled template in VISIO which helps me make BPMN compliant diagrams. However, the users I have dealt with do not know BPMN and hence were not too rigid about the syntax. They were comfortable as long as they understood the diagram. This is one challenge I have seen with standardized modeling notations like BPMN. Unless there is a strong push from organization management or a specific technology need, the acceptance of such notations on the user side becomes challenging. For example, in most of my projects, the stakeholder representative did not care whether I used BPMN notations or not as long as he or she could understand the process flow being depicted. So we need to be very clear on who we are doing it for. If the intent is just to get a business sign-off, then we should just do whatever is easiest for the business to comprehend and understand. If the aim is bigger than that and it's a holistic change of approach on how the specifications are communicated in a standardized way to development teams across the organization, then something like BPMN makes sense.

4) Did use of BPMN add value to your project?

Answer: Before introduction of BPMN the diagrams created by different were not uniform. Each would have his/her own way of depicting process flows with different nomenclature, different iconography and different notations. Practice of BPMN has brought some consistency and standardization to the work of our team. Our documents now look more similar than before. We can maintain common objects repository in tools like iGrafx so that reuse of common components. This also enables management to take an enterprise wide look if required. Additionally, it is easier for the development team to consume the information.

5)   Do you have any experience using Business Process modeling tools? If yes which ones?

> **Answer:** *Say yes to this one only if you have a certain level of exposure to some BPM tool from the several that are available in the market. Most common ones used in the industry are VISIO, TIBCO, Pegasystems, IBM modeler, Sparx Systems Enterprise Architect, HP Process Automation and iGrafx.*

6) A BA team working on a BPM-based project is looking for the right kind of product ranges available for their strategic order processing project. What product options are typically available?

Answer: Typically, BPM products are categorized in the range of integration intensive, automation intensive, human activity intensive, or documentation intensive products. Support for Business Activity Monitoring (BAM) is also a common requirement if reporting is expected to be an important feature. While choosing the right BPM product, all the above mentioned requirements are considered. Additionally, pricing and organizational preference/available licenses need to be considered. For example, BPM products such as Documentum and FileNet are suitable for content-centric requirements, whereas Savvion and Lombardi are better suited for workflow and data intensive processes.

7) What is the difference between BPM process template and instance?

Answer: Process template is the "master" copy of a BPM based process. When an analyst designs a process, it is a process **template**, whereas when the process runs or executes, it is called process **instance**. For example, when the onboarding process has a created structure or template in BPM tool, it is called a process template. For each person undergoing the onboarding process, a fresh new template instance is created, wherein it runs and takes its own path depending on data and conditions associated real time.

8) What is the key benefit of using BPM based process methodology?

Answer: The key benefit is that processes can be defined iteratively while involving stakeholder feedback with active participation. At the end of the iteration, you consolidate and assess process measurement data so that it can be improved in the next iteration. This all fits well into the Agile framework as well. Other key benefits are standardization, visualization, potentially reusable processes, and monitoring of processes real time.

Let me provide a real-life example. In my last project, we had to build a workflow-based application that would monitor the approval process for new technology initiatives. It was a complex process with many players, permutations, and combinations. A very basic flow diagram existed in VISIO that was created by a senior developer who had just left the firm. It only provided a high level sequence of steps but was not adequate to develop the rules engine. Then we decided to use a proper BPM approach with process discovery sessions and documentation in iGrafx and BPMN notations.

There was an immediate improvement in everyone's understanding of the requirements. Many rules that would have gone unnoticed or hidden under heaps of FRD pages were now well understood, easily consumed, and accessible. Creating graphs and score cards for management or even for troubleshooting, which were formerly a full day's job, was now a click of the button, etc.

9)   What are typical elements of Business Activity Monitoring?

Answer: Business Activity Monitoring (BAM) is about real time analysis and monitoring of a process in a BPM suite. Most of the time, it provides a variety of custom dashboards to stakeholders and the KPIs that are important to them along with actual metrics associated with the KPIs. One can even expect scorecards, graphs, and other types of reports in it.

10)   In what situations would a BA who is modeling a BPM-based flow use a "user" type of task showing the associated IT system?

Answer: When all or most of the task is being done through a given IT system, the business analyst would use the IT system as a swim lane, or identify the activity or task as user type wherein a system is being used to perform a task, for example, a data entry person using a specific tool for entering data in the system.

11) If all the BPM tools being proposed for the new automation platform are meeting the requirements, what should a business analyst do to narrow down the choices?

Answer: If all tools seem to be meeting requirements equally, typically a BA or BPM consultant defines parameters for selection and assessment and then goes about scoring each product. A BA may involve various stakeholders from the organization as needed and eventually pick the highest scoring product. Sometimes it is worthwhile to even purchase an industry standard scoring report, such as from Gartner, so that we get an objective assessment in the most reliable manner. Typical parameters for comparison and scoring are process design and deployment capabilities, integration support, performance, cost vs value for the given organization, data or content support, user base, and scalability

12) In which sort of projects would a BA opt for an in-built rule engine within a BPM product as against an external rule engine and rules management system?

Answer: One instance is when rules are relatively simpler, and cost is a consideration. Separate rules management systems can end up being a costlier option. For example, if the rules are around basic tax calculation by slabs, it is recommended to use in-built rules. However, for an advanced system involving thousands of insurance specific rules and policy, it is worthwhile going for a dedicated BRMS (business rules management systems) tool such as Blaze Advisor.

13) **Is there a need to use separate requirements documentation on a BPM project? In other words, is a BPMN-based model, by itself, sufficient to convey the requirements to stakeholders?**

Answer: Yes, many times just BPMN models are insufficient. A project may require BRD, business process list, software requirement specification (SRS), and supporting docs such as state diagrams, and specific use cases to complete the picture. For example, in a sales and fulfillment process, we could have level 1 to 3 diagrams built into process models with every possible detail; however, a dedicated BRD is required by stakeholders to define the scope, assumptions, constraints, etc.

14) **Stakeholders want to see the entire set of processes that are part of the project in one go. What kind of**

models would you create as a BA, in addition to BPMN-based individual process models?

Answer: I would consider creating a level 1 diagram, which is a process landscape to show all processes and key details. It gives an overall set of processes involved very neatly, and many process modeling tools using BPMN support the creation of process landscape. For sponsors and stakeholders that are keen on seeing the summary, it really helps to have a one-stop process landscape with key processes to be addressed and in scope. We can even show out-of-scope processes in it by using different color coding.

Level 2 BPM process is usually a detailed process diagram for each component from level 1., for example, data entry process, underwriting process, etc.

Level 3 BPM process is usually a specific process which is either reusable or detailed and unique enough to be added as level 3., for example, handling a specialized delegation matrix for an underwriting process.

15) Stakeholders are keen on displaying which inputs and outputs are being used for each step in a process. How would you go about clarifying it?

Answer: I'd specify them as input and output for each step and link them correctly to the step. Each task or activity definition can be linked to one or more data inputs /outputs. A BA needs to create data objects first and then mention them as input or output, or both, and then continue with linking activity.

16) In which projects/situations would you, as business analyst, use executable (BPMN) process models?

Answer: Executable process models are very advanced and very few projects would have a need for a BA to directly create executable models. Typically, the Business Process Modelling Notation (BPMN) diagrams I have created have been created to standardize the specifications and communicate the process requirement to the business stakeholder and the development team. With executable models, one can directly generate code and have the system behave as per the rules engine one has created. However, this requires very in-depth knowledge of BPMN, and the syntax has to be perfect. Additionally, the code generated has to be compatible with whatever the choice of underlying software is. This makes the use of executable models very complicated. I would rather use a BPMN tool like Pega or IBM BPM to create the executable model but use regular BPMN notations on iGrafx or VISIO for regular communication.

17) How would you, as business system analyst, working

on a project go about building user groups and translating them to respective swim lanes?

Answer: One approach would be to elicit details around user groups, their roles and responsibilities in the process, the size of each group, and any other relevant info first. Usually these details are created in a separate document such as an Excel spreadsheet or Word document. In the spreadsheet, one can also write additional info such as user authentication. Accordingly, one can go about creating pools and swim lanes for user groups using the BPMN model.

18) In what situations, as a BA, should you opt for BPMN-based models as compared to traditional flow charts, etc.?

Answer: When the industry standard definition of a process is needed, with the possibility of making the processes executable with better visualization, one should definitely use BPMN-based models. Whereas, in other instances, it is even sufficient to just use a standard flow chart. The decision also depends on the organization's readiness to embrace BPM.

19) The process in consideration is being triggered by an inbound B2B transaction. How will it be represented in a BPMN model?

Answer: 'Start task' should be defined as 'event based' and the B2B event and details should be configured there. Event-based triggers are common in a workflow or BPM process. The definition of the trigger needs to be done accurately while also supporting it by additional documentation that defines the B2B data involved, in this case.

20)   Give an example of using parallel gateways in a BPMN model.

Answer: Parallel gateways are created when there are multiple parallel paths in a process. The process will not move forward until all paths are executed. For example, one path describes the process for packing bags, a second path describes the process for packing food, and a third process for preparing travel docs. All of these can be in parallel path; once all are done, one is set for the journey.

21)   A step in a workflow needs information from SAP system which is being used as back-end. What is a possible way in which it can be represented?

Answer: Usually the technical solution is either building a custom adapter which integrates with the SAP system or alternatively, use ready adapters such as IBM Websphere adapter for SAP for integration configuration. For example, a BPM process which uses SAP's sales and order management modules at the back-end and provides interface to support manual intervention and other steps to add missing parts to the process. This requires pulling data back and forth with SAP modules; Websphere SAP adapters come handy in such cases.

22) When would you, as business analyst, consider breaking a process into sub-processes?

Answer: When there is a need for re-use of the tasks within a sub-process or when it is visually getting too detailed and there is a need to break it into parts.

23) Is it a possibility that the actor in a BPMN flow is an individual user? In which situations?

Answer: Yes, this is a possibility in certain projects, especially when light weight processes are involved and names of the actors are in the form of no role, but individualized names.

24) What happens when a process invokes a sub-process? How does the control and data flow? Cite some

examples using sub-processes.

Answer: In this case, control gets transferred to the called process, and it executes per the design. Control then comes back to the calling process. This happens in synchronous processes. For asynchronous, an invoked process may execute its own path and end there. The calling process will move forward as well.

25)   An online customer is provided an option to book flights, as well as flights and hotels. What kind of gateways would you consider using in this case?

Answer: I'd use an OR gateway- One path for flights, and a second path for flights plus hotels. Both of these paths need to be joined using the same OR gateway.

26)   A B2B transaction that was used to trigger the workflow process needs to now show some of the data elements from B2B on the UI. How would you as BA go about building such a UI?

Answer: In this case, the inbound B2B data needs to be mapped to the appropriate UI elements. Actual mapping information may be provided using the BPM tool itself, or additionally, using documents such as mapping specifications or the SRS document that details data and mapping aspects. A mapping diagram may be helpful here as well.

27)   A stakeholder intends to send out an alert if the task is not done in a specific duration. Can this be presented in a BPMN flow? If yes, how?

Answer: Several BPM tools support usage of overdue alerts in such cases. These are usually available in process designer and for each task. There is a provision to configure this kind of trigger alert by stating the duration after which the task becomes overdue.

28)   Advanced BPMS systems allow a provision for some pre activities to be executed in a task. Can you provide some examples when this kind of provision is needed?

Answer: These features typically support data or process validations or define an alert to be sent. For example, the data captured using the screen associated with a task may have to be validated before the task gets executed. These functions are done typically in pre activities.

29)   Can you provide an example wherein a BPM model is useful while defining the software engineering processes?

Answer: Consider review/approve process for requirements specifications or BA deliverables in general. The BA team could come up with an agreeable process wherein it is clear who does what, who is the reviewer, who is the ultimate approver, and how one handles requirements conflicts.

30) A marketing process needs to wait a few days until we send the next email to customers. How would it be represented in a BPMN model?

Answer: BPM tools provide timer step or control. This helps to define the duration/timing aspects related to the delay involved. For example, wait for 1 day after which a follow up email is sent to specific users.

31) What are typical bottleneck areas in an underwriting process?

Answer: Typical bottlenecks in a process are manual tasks, erroneous tasks, unclear rules, and process delays. For instance, an underwriter who processes an application manually is likely to take varied time, plus rules may be unclear or hidden, leading to errors.

32) Typically, how does a business analyst go about adding a user to a role or user group, while using a BPMS system?

Answer: Various methods, including requirements workshops, reviews and creating user /stakeholder charts are helpful in uncovering this list. The PM maybe able to provide detailed stakeholder or user lists himself/herself readily.

33) What is the function of Administration in a typical BPMS system?

Answer: The Admin module of a BPMS system typically involves user group configuration, process start/stop/pause features, and insight into where a process instance is in the flow.

34) How do you plan on preparing for a requirement workshop being planned for global stakeholders to discover level 1 process? What will you ensure so that initial discovery process runs successfully?

Answer: A lot of times, asking for existing documentation, including as-is processes, plus a project vision document, if any, and any rough drafts on to-be processes helps with this phase. Reading all existing documentation, plus having prepared set of initial open questions on processes helps in a great way too.

35) In what situations would you opt for using inclusive

gateway and in which situations would you use exclusive gateway?

Answer: Exclusive gateways are used when two alternatives resulting from a decision are mutually exclusive. For example, payment either by credit card or by net banking. Whereas, if the paths are not mutually exclusive, then an inclusive gateway is useful.

36) What is the difference between pool and lane?
Answer: Pool is a collection of tasks and user groups that logically belong to one process or part of it, for example, the sales fulfillment process could have pools belonging to: 1. order processing; 2. invoicing; and 3. shipment. Lane on the other hand is one section of the pool. A pool is made up of many parallel lanes.

37) When are activities of type 'Send message /Receive message' useful?

Answer: Send message is typically useful when an email or message needs to be sent after completion of an event, say order creation. Receive message is useful when an email or message is to be received or expected at a given instance in a process, for example, receive shipment tracking info.

38) Can you tell something about process discovery

method SIPOC?

Answer: SIPOC is a method which defines components of a process (supplier, input, process, output and customer) which if focused on during process discovery leads to accurate process definition.

39)   What are the different types of challenges you have faced when creating a BPM process diagram involving multiple stakeholders? How did you address those challenges?

Answer: Key challenges in this case are getting them on the same page when it comes to handling especially process overlap areas as well as tackling conflicts around the same. The best approach is to understand each stakeholder's needs individually and see how they fit into overall picture well (business requirements). If there are any inconsistencies, handle them in a timely fashion.   Regular reviews and questionnaire and requirement workshops are necessary in order to achieve this. For example, for a large strategic and global project, an initial requirements workshop with all stakeholder groups present helps immensely to make sure that the process being drawn/built is agreeable to all, before delving into too many details.

40)   What would you do if your business SMEs were neither aware nor interested in BPMN and more

comfortable with regular process flow diagrams?

Answer: Unless there is genuine value in introducing new concepts like BPMN, I would not do it just for the sake of it. However, if I feel the team can benefit from the standardizations that notations like BPMN offer, I would offer to train people on the basics and lead by example so that over time people can start appreciating the benefits. Also, I would explain the change in terms of benefits so that people are not averse to the idea of changing and moving to BPMN.

41)   Give me an overview of how the various diagrams in UML are structured and which ones you are familiar with.

Answer: There are 13 different diagrams in UML 2.0 which are classified into various categories as listed below.

- Behavior Diagrams
- Interaction Diagrams
- Structure Diagrams

Behavior Diagrams are of three categories, and I am well versed with Use Case diagram and activity diagram.

- Use Case Diagram
- Activity Diagram

- State Machine Diagram

Interaction Diagrams are of four types.

- Sequence Diagram
- Communication Diagram
- Timing Diagram
- Interaction Overview Diagram

Structure Diagrams are of 6 types. I have minimal exposure to them as they are used mostly by developers. Package Diagram

- Deployment Diagram
- Object Diagram
- Component Diagram
- Class Diagram
- Composite Structure Diagram

8. BA tasks Related to Software Quality Assurance

1) **As a BA, have you been involved in testing? If yes, to what degree and what process did you adopt to define testing policy?**

Answer: I have been very closely involved in testing right from my first project and understand the process very well. I am not a QA, so I do not have hands-on exposure on automated testing tools. However, for functionality testing, the first line of defense is always a BA. I have done everything from creating test strategy to writing test cases to test execution and supporting UAT very closely. Important steps to formulate a testing policy are provided below, but it can change according to your project needs.

Definition

My first step is always to designate one unique definition for testing within the organization; this way everyone is on the same page.

Execution

Next, I determine how my team will achieve our objective. This includes determining whether there will be a testing committee, defining compulsory test plans which need to be executed, etc.

Evaluation

After testing is implemented in the project, I determine how we will evaluate the same. Among my considerations is whether we will derive metrics of defect per phase, per programmer, etc. I also make sure to let everyone know how testing has added value to the project.

Standards

Finally, I look at the standards we want to achieve by testing. For instance, we can say that more than 20 defects per KLOC will be considered below standard and code review should be done for the same.

2)   What is the usual approach that you take when preparing test cases?

Answer: I try to first map the high level scope items to requirements to use cases. If we are following the Agile approach, then I look at the user stories. Once I do this I try to come up with as many test cases as possible and map them back to the use cases or user stories. In doing so, my attempt is to first cover basic cases and then to go to unique cases which can break the system. Additionally, I always keep a set of regression test cases ready for end to end, or sanity testing. This way, I am able to test for a combination of individual functionality and end to end functions.

3)   What has been your involvement in UAT?

Answer: I'm involved in UAT end to end and often drive the entire effort.

Providing inputs into the UAT plan, helping out the users in conducting UAT, issue tracking and resolution during UAT, and getting sign off from users.

4)   Did you create or facilitate the creation of UAT test plans on behalf of business users?

Answer: I always have a plan for SIT (System Integration Testing). I often offer this to the users so they can leverage it to come up with a UAT test plan. However, the actual UAT plan is always prepared by a user as they might have some specific user based perspectives that I might miss if I do it in isolation.

However, I do oversee the UAT and ensure that issues are classified as either bugs or enhancements. If an issue is an enhancement, I also make sure that it goes back in the addendum of a FRD (for Waterfall) or a product backlog user story (for Agile).

5)   What are the different categories that you would typically use to classify defects?

Answer: Typically, I would use the following categories to classify defects:
Urgent
These are the defects that completely prevent us from moving forward with testing until they are resolved.   For example, if I am building a process-based application and the basic step of the process is not working in the system that is an urgent defect.

High

These are important requirements which, if not met, will prevent the application from being released into production. For example, there is an automated email feature which was clearly listed as a requirement. Assume this is not working. This does not mean that the process cannot move forward. However, the client will not release the application without fixing this. Hence, it's not an urgent defect, but its resolution is a high priority.

Medium

When a requirement which is nice to have, but not critical to the process, fails, then the defect can be classified as low. For example, if a particular report is not being sorted properly, but displays the correct data, then it is a medium defect. It's an irritant for user experience, but there is nothing fundamentally wrong with it.

Low

A low defect is typically for things like aesthetics, incorrect grammar or spelling, and items related to display. Ideally, all types of defects should be fixed before releasing a product into production, but low defects can possibly become a book of work for the next release if there is a time crunch.

6)   What are some common problems you have observed in projects that might make testing challenging? Also provide ways in which you have overcome these

challenges.

<u>Answer</u>: Some common problems in the software development process that might make testing challenging are:

Inaccurate or incomplete requirements:

There are many reasons why requirements can be inaccurate or incomplete, and this directly affects the development and subsequently, the testing. Sometimes the requirements might not be at a level of detail to tie back to granular test cases. In such situations, the test team has to take the best guess on what the outcome of a test case should be.
This can become ambiguous and problematic when the product goes to UAT. To resolve this, a tester should also behave like a BA. Whenever you find a requirement where a clear test case cannot be defined, or insufficient detail is available, you should speak up and ask the BA to get the missing information. This will consume time but will make sure that the product you deliver is what the users really want.

Non-functional requirements provided by the BA

This is a very common problem in many projects. Functional requirements are obvious, thus most of the time is spent eliciting them. Nonfunctional requirements are not directly visible to end users and are neglected during requirement gathering sessions. However, they are very important for rolling out a good product. Therefore, when nonfunctional requirements are not provided, it is indirectly a case of missing requirements. To overcome this situation, I would typically ask around to determine what the nonfunctional expectations have been in other equivalent projects in the company. I would test for at least the key nonfunctional requirements based on my knowledge of equivalent projects, especially from a user experience perspective.

Unrealistic schedule

I've been involved with many projects where the time allocated for any phase, including testing, is reverse-engineered based on a nonnegotiable end date defined by management. This leads to unrealistic schedules and a short time allocated for testing. There are ways to handle this. One way is to ensure that the test cases are clearly prioritized so that we can test out the high and medium cases first. Alternatively, we can also do less documentation and more ad hoc testing to cover the key features of the system in the time that has been provided.

Inadequate planning for testing

There are many aspects that must be planned thoroughly, well in advance of the first test case being executed. Some of these are as follows:
- Timeline
- How will knowledge transition happen?
- Which different functional and nonfunctional dimensions will be tested?
- What will the daily process be?
- What kind of mock data is required, and how will it be produced?
- What will each individual's role be?
- What entitlements and accesses are required before we can start?

- What potential impediments exist?

7)   Give me examples of how you would test different types of functional and non-functional requirements.

Answer: *This question will usually not be asked in one go. The interviewer might go over different types of functional and non-functional requirements separately and ask you to provide examples of each. The answer provided below is a compilation of all of that put together.*

Most systems are defined by the following types of **functional requirements**. The application purpose, users, size, complexity, etc. might be different but any software system has the following types of functional features:

User interface

This is the key aspect of any system because it is the only visible part of the system to the end users. Typically, the requirements are captured in the form of detailed wireframes or high-level screen design. The testing includes ensuring that the interface meets all the specifications defined as per the wireframe, testing whether the navigations work as per the process flows, and ensuring the various fields of the data capture on online forms are as per what has been specified in the data dictionary.

Data

This is another very important part of any system. Though not directly visible to an end user, it manifests itself in many forms including the data that is captured by a system or data that is displayed on the user interface. Testing includes checking the fields of the UI against the data type, size limitations, permissible values, and business rules around the display as specified in the data dictionary. In some projects where you move from an old system to a new system, there might also be an element of data migration involved.

This is usually very challenging to test, as the mapping between the old system and the new system is sometimes complex. Testing data mapping typically involves taking a production cut into UAT or QA and comparing the old data with the new to ensure there is no data loss.

Process flow

The sequence of steps that a user has to take to accomplish a particular business objective is the crux of most applications. There can be one or more types of flows within an application. Testing involves ensuring that the rules of the process flow are working properly and a user is able to go through the process end to end without problems.

Onboarding and entitlements In any application, a user needs to be on-boarded before he/she can use the system. Additionally, after being on-boarded, there are rules around what a person can or cannot do or see in the system.

Not everyone has all privileges. For example, after you log into Gmail, you can only see your inbox and not anyone else's. This is the concept of entitlement, and it's very important to test it during QA. This has a direct bearing on the security of the system, hence it is important that the testers log in as different roles and confirm whether the entitlements are working properly.

Reports and dashboards

Most applications have some form of reporting available. It can be simple query-based reports, static reports, customizable reports, or complex visual infographics on dashboards.

The various things a tester can check in reporting include whether the column structure is correct, whether the query results in the correct data being produced in the report, whether the infographic is created as specified, and whether the entitlements of the report are working properly. Regression testing should also be conducted with older versions to make sure nothing is broken.

Interface with other systems

No system is an island unto itself. In most projects, you work with upstream and downstream systems that share data with you. The various things you can test with regard to external system interfaces include live feeds, testing whether the correct data is sourced or given to the external system, whether the interface method (e.g., web service call or batch file) is working properly, etc.

Other automated functionality

There are many bells and whistles in a system, such as automated emails, automated system tasks, automated error messages, system update messages, administration functionalities, etc. When testing the process flow, a good tester will also test all the related functionality at each step of the process as per the specifications document. For example, if a particular step in the process flow is supposed to trigger automated emails, then as a tester, I will check the email completely, including the audience it triggers, the subject, the body, and the timing.

Additionally, there are **non-functional requirements**. These are more challenging to test than the functional ones. This is because non-functional requirements are not directly visible to an end user and are not as easily quantifiable. Some non-functional requirements and the ways in which I can test them are as follows:

Performance

This is the most important nonfunctional requirement, as it directly relates to user experience. Some of the testing involves system response for various actions like logging in, submission of online forms, running reports, and other navigational steps.

Usability

Usability is about how easy the system feels for a user. There are several things such as intuitiveness, UI design, number of lines on a page, number of rows in reports, how easily you are able to find functions on the UI, color combinations, ease of navigation, etc. Tests can be created based on the specific items listed out in the FRD document, and some ad hoc testing can be performed based on your past experience.

Data retention, availability, and recovery

Most systems have very clear requirements for how long data should be stored, the maximum amount of data permissible, the disaster recovery parameters, the recovery time, and recovery point objective, etc.

Testing these things is very challenging and needs to be done separately. It's called DR testing (disaster recovery) and involves a complex orchestration of having a parallel server where your code is maintained, shutting down the main server, and testing whether the application can still function with the DR server. This is a simplified explanation, but there are a lot more steps involved.

Capacity and user base

This is called load testing and usually involves automation. Typically, requirements specifications have details on what kind of user base is expected, what the growth will be, and the number of transactions it will process.

Testing involves simulating the peak loads in terms of users logging in and also simultaneous transactions happening on the system.

Security

System security is a complex subject and is highly critical. Main types of security requirements generally include confidentiality, entitlements, authentication process, access control, and internal code vulnerabilities. Testing can include manual testing of entitlements or automation by static and dynamic code scans, integrity of third party applications used in the code, security audits, and risk reviews. Additionally, you may also want to perform penetration testing where a malicious code is simulated and tries to get into your database.

Compatibility

This focuses on which types of hardware and software a system should be compatible with. To test this, I would run the application on various computers, on different browsers, on different mobile devices, with different resolutions, etc., and check to see if my user experience is consistent.

8)   What are some of the things you typically put on a QA report?

Answer: QA reports can range from very basic to very fancy, but they usually have two fundamental types of data:

Test coverage

This provides information on the percentage of test cases completed per category. You may want to divide the testing into various functional and nonfunctional categories based on what makes sense in that project. Test cases are written for each category, so we need to provide information daily on what percentage of test cases have been completed.

Defect statistics

This provides the number of urgent, high, medium, and low defects found per category. A combination of coverage and the number of defects tells us how well the QA effort is progressing and how clean the code is. Additionally, I also like to have a detailed defect log which provides a summary of defect description, the status and lifecycle of each defect, the owner, the finder, any attachments, approximate fix date, and priority of the defect. HP ALM can be used to produce these reports and manage the test cycles.

9)   Please walk me through the daily activities you go through when a testing cycle is ongoing.

Answer: All organizations have slightly different approaches to the testing process, but the fundamental steps are:

- It all starts with lots of planning and requirements understanding. Details are worked out with the development team around different categories of tests required, code coverage, roles of people, timing of activities, creation of dummy data, access and environment preparation, etc.

- Then the actual test execution begins. During execution, we meet with the offshore and onsite development teams first thing every morning to go over the highlights of the defects found during the previous day.

- During this meeting, we do defect triaging, as well as classifying the defect and explaining why we think it's a defect.

- The rest of the day is spent testing the various items assigned to each team member. Each person updates ALM, or any equivalent system, immediately upon finding a bug. There is a possibility the same bug will be found by multiple people. The offshore development team removes such duplications.

- At the end of the day, there is an internal QA team meeting to discuss the bugs found and the progress for that day.

- The offshore team extracts reports from ALM to take

a look at the bugs we've found. They plan defect fixes for bugs that are well understood and mark the ones they have questions about. These are discussed in the next morning's meeting, and the same cycle continues until the end of QA.

10) What would you do if, in the middle of the testing cycle, it was observed that there are too many significant bugs which cannot be resolved in the allotted time?

<u>Answer</u>: I have worked on projects where there were too many bugs in the software and very little time left for resolution. When we plan the start and end date for the QA effort, we do not have the benefit of hindsight. The assumption is that the software is reasonably bug-free and that development has done system integration tests based on signed-off requirements. However, this is sometimes easier said than done, as development is also under a lot of stress to deliver and might not have had a chance to go over unit or system testing thoroughly.

So in situations where we start testing and there are too many bugs, it's a big problem because each bug has to be fixed and retested. The turnaround from the development team might not be fast enough to meet deadlines. In such situations, there are a few things we can do:

• Allow the code into UAT with certain known defects

that can be designated as enhancements later. This depends on the severity of the bugs. If there are too many urgent or high defects, then this is not possible.

• Determine whether the application can be repackaged in order to enable a partial release instead of full release.

• Extend the timeline formally and spend more time in defect fixes. This is sometimes the only way out if there are too many urgent and high defects with no workarounds, no remediation, or time to fix. It's the last resort and will reflect badly on the project, but sometimes it is necessary.

11) What are the main contents you would include in a test strategy if you are creating it?

Answer: The test strategy is a company-level document the template for which is typically recommended by the PMO or an equivalent shared-services group. It is then customized for the project by the test manager based on the unique considerations for the particular application. The typical things I would include in a test strategy document are:

• Types of testing
• Steps that we need to complete before testing
• The testing approach, including details like number of users, creation of test cases, execution approach, ownership, etc.
• QA timelines
• Testing process with actors and daily steps

- Documents to be prepared with respective formats

12) How would you get the maximum output from an offshore team?

Answer: To get the maximum output, I would do the following:
- Involve everyone in test case reviews, NOT only the module owner.
- Involve everyone in knowledge transfer sessions, regardless of who is working on which module.
- Avoid too much dependence on one resource.
- Capture all the requirement-related clarification in the application management tool.
- Avoid email clarification on requirements or defects.
- Ensure that any clarification given on any defect through email is also captured in the defect management tool.
- Constantly encourage the concept of teamwork.

13) How do you deal with the situation where a high severity defect is found in the last few hours of testing?

Answer: I begin by explaining the situation to the client. If I have a valid reason why the high severity defect escaped my attention in early testing, then I'll explain that too. I'll make sure I explain the consequences of releasing the product with that defect. I'll involve developers to discuss the time needed to fix the defect.

Also, the impact of the defect/bug should be analyzed, and one should try to find workarounds for the defect. This should be listed in the release notes as known issues, known limitations, or known bugs.

I can provide one example from a recent project. This was a process flow application where one of the screens involved an online form called 'Finance team considerations'. The finance team had provided a more recent version to the BA to add as part of the requirement, but it was missed for some reason. During testing, we found out that the implementation was slightly different from the latest version of the Word template for 'Finance team considerations' that was provided to us. We raised this as a high severity defect. After discussion with the business, we agreed that the time left was not sufficient to fix it before production. Instead, we provided a workaround for the first release where the application had an upload feature instead of an online form for 'Finance team considerations'. We provided the actual online form in the next release.

14)   How do you determine whether the number of test cases created covers the functionality completely?

Answer: The BA should create a requirement traceability matrix. This document provides direct traceability between the business requirements and the functional specifications and user cases (or user stories in Agile). When we get to the test case preparation, we should make sure that each test case aligns directly with one or more user cases so it becomes a continuation of the traceability matrix. Most of my projects have had between 400 to 1000 test cases.

15)   What should be the approach when there is very little time given for testing, and you have to complete the testing within that short time frame?

Answer:

•   Ad hoc testing always yields good results in less time. The key here is to assign different areas of the application to different team members to perform ad hoc testing.
•   Execute sanity and smoke test cases.
•   Check with the BA and developers to decide on the high priority test cases. Execute high priority test cases first.

16)   What are the problems a tester can face if (s)he uses only the Software Requirement Specification (SRS)

document as a basis for testing?

Answer: SRS or FRD, if well written, can be an excellent start to thinking about the positive scenarios. However, there may be some complex scenarios which need to be tested but cannot be understood by just reading the SRS. In such a case, a tester needs to understand the whole functionality from the development team or project manager. If there are issues, (s)he must confirm by performing the scenario practically.

9. BA in Agile Projects

This section will cover some real life practical questions about managing Agile projects. This is not an Agile training so we assume that you are well versed with most of the basic concepts of Agile SDLC. We build on that assumption and elaborate questions that talk to different aspects of an agile implementation.

1) Have you ever been involved in a major Agile transformation from Waterfall? Describe your experience.

Answer: My latest project started off as Waterfall, but the company decided to adopt Agile in the middle of it and for all projects going forward.

Since the project started as Waterfall, we spent a lot of time documenting the details around requirements. We had a full suite of documentation including BRD, FRD, tech design, etc. We also had lots of details like process models, data models, and functional and non-functional requirements in the FRD.

The project was developed on time and everything seemed to be on track. There were some issues with too many bugs found during QA, but it was easily overcome. When we moved the product to UAT, we were very confident that we had completed everything successfully and were already patting ourselves on the back. Little did we know that a huge surprise awaited us. This was a cross-organizational application, so a central team had signed off on requirements.

The actual users of the system had only taken a cursory look at the documents. Additionally, documents never do the justice that a real product can. Hence the users started giving actual feedback only after we provided them the UAT link. The result was a disaster.

Change after change was requested, and many fundamental things had to be rewritten. This resulted in a lot of wasted time, and the project got delayed. By this time, the firm was also mandating Agile practice for all major projects. We thought this was a good opportunity to jump on the Agile bandwagon. In hindsight, we should have adopted Agile for our project from the beginning. We decided to do it for phase two.

It was a culture change not only for I.T. but also for the business side. I took on the role of a scrum master, and the BAs assumed the product owner role. The first thing we did was create a proper product backlog based on the use cases that we had documented in the first phase. These epics and user stories were uploaded into Rally where we now maintain them.

The next step was to have an iteration zero where we went over high-level requirements of what was needed in phase 2. We did have some basic documentation - enough to get started. Agile does not mean NO documentation, it merely means MINIMUM documentation.

Based on our iteration zero discussions, we started the sprint planning. We decided that 4-week sprints worked best for us with 1 week of requirement fine tuning, 2 weeks of development, and 1 week of testing each sprint.

Instead of long, verbose FRDs, we now maintain process models in iGrafx. The process models also contain details of the business rules. One of the BAs became a UX consultant. We try to have mock screens in Axure so that requirements are modeled visually and we can react quickly to changes.

I had to change the way that I capture project progress. I still provide the standard weekly RAG reporting, monthly budget reports, and other management reports, but all I care about for the sprints are the burn up and burn down charts. I have formatted the data in a particular way to get this information, and it makes it easy to follow and incredibly useful.

We do a telephonic daily standup, as many team members are offshore, but it works well for us.

All in all, Agile has worked very well for us as we are more adaptive to change and have faster error-free deliveries. True, it does not lend itself to pure technology endeavors like tech refresh, server upgrades, software upgrades, and pure data migration projects. However, it has worked very well for regular projects, especially where business user interaction is involved.

2) Typically, context diagrams provide a context for the application's ecosystem in Waterfall. Do we need tools like context diagrams or state transition diagrams in Agile?

If not, then how do developers know these details? For example, I'm working on a process flow project. This is an approval process flow where an initiative goes from creation state to fully approved state. There are many states in between, and there is value in knowing what trigger moves an initiative from one state to the next. How would I have shown this in Agile if there was no documentation?

Answer: Scrum framework does not "ban" documentation, it just states that working software is more important. That said, if the scrum team sees value in building a context diagram, they should do so. It can be an ongoing effort, and there can be multiple user stories for it in separate sprints. The idea behind Scrum and Agile is to focus on working software immediately. In Waterfall development, we would start actual software development without having multiple artifacts first (e.g., requirements doc, architecture doc, use cases, etc.). Scrum does not "ban" any of these artifacts if the Scrum Team and stakeholders see value in having them. Scrum simply states that development can start without having all these documents prepared. Indeed, for smaller projects (e.g., mobile apps and websites), teams usually do not produce all the documentation required for larger, enterprise systems. Once again, it is all a matter of planning and cost-benefit ratio.

3) How exactly is wireframing done in Agile? Sometimes wireframes are all-or-nothing. Unless I have a holistic picture of how the system is going to work, it's very difficult for me to create it piece by piece. In Agile, however, there won't be time to create the entire wireframe. What then is the approach in Agile?

Answer: The main difference between Agile and Waterfall, in this case, would be that in Waterfall, we would spend 6 months wireframing the product and defining every single functionality and use case and wouldn't start with development until the whole wireframe was done. In Agile, we would spend the first sprint or two working on the prototype, that is, the basic conceptualization of the product.

For example, let's say we were building an e-commerce application. We would start with a basic wireframe that will reflect what screens we think our application will have for each of the user roles we want.

Example

Interface that end users will see:
- Landing page
- List of products page
- Single product page
- Shopping cart

- Payment process

First, we would do a low-fidelity prototype that would not go into details of what each screen would contain.
After finishing general wireframe, we would focus on each screen at the time and work toward a high-fidelity prototype. If we had the luxury of doing user testing or discussing our prototype with the client, we would iterate and change our design to best fit user/client needs before starting development.
This would minimize the chance that we are building something completely wrong and is a basic principle of the Agile development – getting feedback and being on the right track. We would not predict every possible use case, but at this point, the client would have a pretty good idea what our application will look like and what will be its most important features. The main takeaway here is that there will be some trial and error, but that is the beauty of Scrum and Agile. Since we are working in short iterations (i.e., sprints), we are able to rapidly respond to changes in demands.

In Waterfall, the data models are critical to success. The developer will never be able to create the correct product unless I provide a detailed conceptual data model which specifies the attributes of each data element on the UI and on the backend. Additionally, if they are migrating data from an older system to a newer system they will

absolutely need the mapping. However, I have never heard of detailed work being done on the data side in Agile.

4) How are requirements around data captured in Agile? Please explain with examples.

<u>Answer</u>: In Agile, the main difference is that you are always (first) thinking from the user perspective. In this case, you would create a user story describing what the user can accomplish and then you would add acceptance criteria that can include details regarding the data model.

Since Scrum Teams are independent, there is no separate architecture team or team member assigned to architecture. Everything is decided within the Scrum Team.

Most importantly, things change. Scrum Team members have a lot more autonomy, and the team is responsible for all results.

If the Product owner sees value in describing a data model within a user story/acceptance criterion, then so be it.

In the case of data migration, we can:

• Have an epic called "Migration" where we will describe everything that needs to be migrated, or

- We can create multiple user stories that will follow the development of functionalities that will depend on certain data being migrated.

5) How would you capture non-functional requirements in Agile?

Answer: Scrum Teams have a set of rules/artifacts that are applicable to every item/JIRA ticket the Scrum team delivers. This is called "Definition of Done" (DoD) and is considered a part of every single artifact/feature/item that Scrum Teams deliver.

Initial DoD is usually developed in the first sprint (or Sprint 0 if the team needs to have it). DoD evolves and expands as Scrum Teams work more and more together and add stricter quality standards.

All non-functional requirements need to be a part of the DOD criteria.

6) How do you capture the production support process and the enhancement request process in Agile style development?

Answer: When doing sprint planning, teams usually set aside a certain amount of capacity for unexpected production issues, support, etc. Teams use various techniques when estimating work (story points, working hours, etc.). What I typically do with my teams is plan for a 13-point "Sustainment & Maintenance" JIRA user story where team members capture all these urgent tasks, as well as other tasks that are not part of other sprint work. The important thing is that we allocate time for this.

7) In Agile, what does one do in cases of data-driven projects, infrastructure projects, legacy modernization projects, or tech refresh projects? How do you have user stories in these areas?

Answer: Scrum is not a silver bullet. For example, even support teams that want to practice Agile usually go with Kanban instead of Scrum. Every project has its specifics, and Scrum is not an ideal solution for every type of project. One must think through carefully on the intended objectives and the capacity to adapt to change before deciding to go for SCRUM-based SDLC.

8) What happens when you realize in the middle of a sprint that you cannot deliver? Do you call off the sprint or do you deliver regardless? Give detailed examples.

Answer: This is a common question, and the first problem I see is with the wording "cannot deliver". Since Scrum is all about responding to change and delivering work in chunks, sprints should always have a sprint goal. Sprint goal is defined during the sprint planning and usually represents the main features (i.e., the most important items that will come out of that sprint).

That said, these items are usually worked on first because they need to be delivered for the sprint work to be demoed and the sprint to be considered successful. Ideally, you should not have make-or-break features (i.e., a build should be deliverable with the features that are working). If there is a high-risk feature that we are unsure will fit in a single sprint, we usually start working on it on a separate branch and merge it only when we feel comfortable.

The product owner has the authority to cancel sprints if they no longer make sense (i.e., if the circumstances have changed so much that finishing the sprint as it was planned just doesn't bring any value).

In worst-case scenarios where the team estimate and commitment were so off that you have nothing to show, the product owner needs to go before the stakeholders and call that particular sprint a failure.

9) How exactly is testing planned and executed in Agile? Without adequate test documentation, how do you

populate test cases into ALM? And if it cannot be in a tool like ALM, how you do ensure adequate coverage?

Answer: ALM test cases can be a part of the Scrum Team's 'Definition of Done' (i.e., team members would write and maintain them). In larger-scale projects, you will need some way to track test coverage. In smaller projects, automated test scripts are usually what gives you an idea of system coverage.

Testing/QA is an integral part of every user story/feature. A feature is not delivered until it's thoroughly tested. If the acceptance criteria and/or DOD also requires test cases in a test case management tool - so be it. Once again, Agile enables us to respond to change. Agile doesn't see value in writing every possible test case before we have a piece of working software because the assumption is that the software will change and evolve as the user and/or stakeholder needs it to evolve.

10)   What are all the things that you should cover in iteration zero? How long does iteration zero typically last?

Answer: Iteration 0 or sprint 0 lasts one sprint (sprint length is usually 1-4 weeks, 2 weeks being most common). Sprint 0 is usually used by teams that haven't worked together before to set up some infrastructure (code repository, hardware, initial DOD etc.). It is called sprint 0 since teams do not usually deliver working software out of this iteration.

11) How do you decide what is a minimum viable product? What if the product is all-or-nothing, like regulatory applications where you cannot have half of a regulation fulfilled?

Answer: The product owner is responsible for optimizing the value of the work that the Scrum Team does. That said, he or she steers the team toward the MVP and decides what the MVP is. For regulatory applications, Scrum is probably not the best method to use.

While you can make Scrum work for these projects, they have some characteristics that are just not natural to Scrum (e.g., very strict deadlines, documentation and project scope needs to be agreed in advance, etc.).

12) In Agile projects, how do you decide when an implementation is over and when the project is in BAU mode? Where does the project end and enhancement request begin?

Answer: At the end of every sprint, the Product Owner decides if the build should be deployed to production. The team is responsible for making a potentially shippable increment, but the Product Owner decides if and when to release it to production.

At the end of the day, it depends on the type of project, users, and other teams (e.g., sales, marketing, etc.). For example, if you are building a B2C product and have an assumption you want to validate, you will go to production very early (as soon as possible). At other times, you want to build a complete solution and then release it to users.

Even though you are doing the core software development in a new framework (Scrum), there are still other factors and marketplace rules for releasing products that influence decisions like this one.

13) What is the end-to-end cycle of a user story?

Answer: User story is a concept where we capture the requirements using user personas and how they would interact with the system. These are leaner than use cases and are captured in card (main title), conversation (few steps to describe the interaction), and confirmation (definition of what is success). Each story has points that are based on Fibonacci series numbers on relative importance. This is decided informally by the scrum team and the group of user stories is called Epics. The typical steps that also align with the end-to-end cycle of user stories that I have used in my projects is as follows:

- The team starts by brainstorming about the product that we need to build, and we all come up with as many user stories as we can. The level of granularity needs to be determined so there is consistency. We also try to functionally divide the product so there is minimal repetition of stories.

• The team gets together and compiles a final list that is validated by the product owner who is usually from the business side.

• The team then takes the fine-tuned product backlog and adds details like story points and clarifies questions, if any.

• After this, there is some iteration and release planning where we decide which stories should be released when.

• After this starts the regular spring cycle where the user story is developed, tested and put into production, if all goes well. Otherwise, it goes back into product backlog with changes and the cycle keeps repeating till we have a complete product.

10. BA Involvement in Software Build and Deploy

Business systems analysts can be technical or non-technical. Most BA roles do not require hands-on knowledge of technology but expect a familiarity with the software development life cycle and the various software implementation activities at a concept level.

The questions in this section revolve more around the build release and implementation activities. Technology architecture is excluded because it is a very case-specific subject and can be completely different based on the platform, tool, or programming language, and BAs are not expected to have input into technology architectures.

1) What are the responsibilities of application development managers you work with?

<u>Answer:</u>

- Working with the technology architect to ensure that the right architectural considerations are made
- Considering development escalations and resolving them
- Working on the release calendar and ensuring that all internal and external groups needed for successful release are aware of the expectation
- Overseeing production support and enhancement management for applications
- Overseeing all hardware and software requirements of the project
- Owning the entire ITSM (Information Technology Service Management) process for all the major and minor releases
- Ensuring that development best practices are followed by the team
- Ensuring completion of administrative tasks, such as managing details of team members, static and dynamic scans related to application risk, access to integrated development environments, functional IDs, configuration management, etc.
- Ensuring correct details of the application are available in the application directory

2) What were some of the main shared services groups you would interact with as a part of your BA role?

Answer: Some groups that I had to interact with daily were:

Technology infrastructure: This group considers the software and hardware needs of the firm. If you want software licenses, space on a physical server, a share of a cloud server, or access to liquid infrastructure, this is the group you consult.

Operate: This group typically assists with any access to the servers. Usually, in large companies, there are strict restrictions on who can access production data and/or servers directly. The operate group acts as a layer to help you with any activity that requires server access, like getting data logs or usage logs for analysis, letting you know whether software processing or hardware capabilities have hit upper limits, or moving code from one environment to another during releases.

Development office: This shared group typically makes recommendations or mandates on the development best practices and/or the tools to use.

Shared services groups: Often peripheral or transient tasks, such as software quality assurance, business analysis, process consulting, IT risk consulting, or data center of excellence, are not performed by dedicated members of your team. The tasks are performed by centralized shared teams whose members are loaned to your project only on an as-needed basis. You need to interact with such shared service groups based on the demands of your projects.

All companies have some variation of the groups listed above, and typically, all these groups also have some in-house applications that they use to provide service to different projects. A BA acting as the application development manager needs to be familiar with the groups and their respective applications.

3) Can you describe the typical ITSM (I.T. Service Management) process you follow for your releases?

<u>Answer</u>:

• Typically, we create ITSM entries in an in-house system 2 weeks before the release. This entry includes a lot of detail on the features of the release, who is required, timing, etc.
• The plans written in the ITSMs must be reviewed in detail.

- The various plans inside the ITSM must be approved by various parties.
  - E.g. implementation plans, roll back plans, results of static and dynamic application scans, UAT signoff emails, and other such evidence of completion.
- Releases usually happen on Friday after business hours so that application usage is not affected.

4) Can you describe the typical enhancement management process you follow once your project is in BAU mode?

Answer: Once the initial rollout of the product is completed, I generally follow these steps for enhancement management:

- Collect, compile, and prioritize the enhancement requests from during and after UAT.
- Enter all requests in an enhancement management system, like JIRA, RALLY, etc.
- Hold sessions with the business and technology teams to discuss exact prioritization. Prioritization typically depends primarily on business urgency, availability of a workaround, ease of implementation, and resource availability.
- The technology team bundles the enhancements using all of the above factors into releases (either sprint releases if it's Agile or regular ad hoc releases if methodology is not that well defined).

- Each release then goes through its development cycle and the product keeps getting upgraded.

5) What kind of production support models are you familiar with?

Answer: Production support is a key activity after the initial launch. I have managed large support teams for many complex projects. Sometimes I am given a shared service team that is exclusively meant for production support, while other times we use members of the development team to manage support. On occasion, it is a mix of the two.

Typically, if it's a smaller project/product with a smaller user base and less criticality, it will suffice to have just a few members of the original development team managing support. This works because the developers are not only familiar with the code, but also know the business functionality very well.

However, for complex cross-functional and cross-organizational projects/products, this is not adequate. We need a much greater division of labor for such critical products.

Usually, the level 1 support will be someone from the business side who is very familiar with the processes and also knows the product. Any issues the users encounter go to this group first. Level 2 support consists of production support professionals. Typically, I have the BA and other subject matter experts train the production support staff in nuances of the business functionality and the code structure. We also use systems like JIRA or Alacrity to automate the support process. Any items raised by the users that the level 1 team considers a production issue are handed over to the level 2 team via an entry into the production support system.

The level 2 team then analyzes the issue and classifies it as a training, performance, data, or functionality issue. Based on the type of issue, it is routed to the appropriate person in level 3 support. Level 3 is the actual developer who can resolve the issue and close the ticket.

The entire life cycle of an issue is tracked by the tool, and updates are provided to everyone involved. There are different resolution times permissible based on agreed SLAs of high, medium, and low items. Most production support tools come with full reporting capabilities, so I keep track of recurrence patterns. This gives me an idea over time of where the problem areas lie and how things can be made more efficient by tackling the root cause.

6) Why do you think we need DevOps?

Answer: The ultimate objective of all I.T. service providers, regardless of whether they are internal or external providers, is customer satisfaction. DevOps helps achieve that end goal in the following ways:

- Reduces failure in new releases
- Ensures better frequency of deployment
- Facilitates reduced recovery time if failure does happen

7) Is DevOps the same as Agile?

Answer:

No.

Agile is an overall software development methodology. It will provide guidelines on all aspects of development from requirements management to production release. It has nothing to do with the technical aspect of build and release or deployment.

DevOps is specifically a concept which deals with integrating the functions of the development team and the operate team during the build, deployment, and release management of code.

8) Can you provide a quick overview of the build and deploy process when you release software?

<u>Answer</u>:

While this may vary from organization to organization, a generic example is:

- Developers write code and it is managed by Version Control System tools like Git SVN.
- Any changes made in the code must be committed to this repository.
- A continuous integration tool like Jenkins pulls this code from the repository using the Git plugin and builds it using build automation tools like Ant or Maven.
- Configuration management tools like Puppet deploy code on the testing environment.
- Continuous integration tools like Jenkins release the code on the test environment.
- Test automation tools like Selenium do the automated testing.
- After testing, Jenkins sends it for deployment on the production server.
- Post-deployment code is continuously monitored by tools like Nagios.

11. Scenario-Based Questions for a BA

1)   How would you handle a situation where your personal opinion on a particular task is radically different from all the other members of a team?

Answer: I would first try and understand the reason for their having that particular opinion and evaluate the expertise of the people that have it. Second, I would introspect and objectively evaluate the reasons for my having a different opinion. Doing so will ensure my opinion is not because of lack of knowledge or prejudices.

After this, if there is very good reason to stick to my opinion, I will; and if not, I'll change. For example, in a recent project where we were trying to move from Mellon Bank to Fidelity as the equity plan administrator for the company, there was a lot of chaos in the start and no one really had a plan of how to move ahead with the project. So they would schedule sessions to discuss the subject matter in general without using any specific method to capture the info and move ahead.

When I proposed that we use actual examples of employee scenarios to capture all that we want, my proposal met with some resistance as people said it's best to just talk and get warmed up before we move ahead with specifics. However, after convincing my managers and peers that to move forward we will need to draft up specific examples, people decided to let me drive one session as a pilot it was successful and people involved saw the value.

Use similar examples from your resume projects.

2)   **Can you provide instances of where you were able**

to think of a solution that nobody else could think of?

Answer: *This is an extremely case-specific question with no generic answer and hence it's best to quote examples from your resume.*

Innovation can happen at various levels and dimensions. Customize your answer based on the following types of innovations:

• Introducing a new BA best practice that never existed before
• Automating a process that used to be done manually
• Suggesting a design solution that saves time and cost by reducing redundancies in the system
• Gathering knowledge on areas that were not explored before

3)   Provide an example of how you handled a situation where the client insisted on implementing a solution that was not practical

Answer: Well, I was in such situation a couple of times at least. With my technical background, I was aware it was not practical to implement the client's request within the given time frame. Without debating their request, I tried suggesting alternative options to address the business problem and slowly made them aware of the feasibility of different alternatives within different time frames, and the client agreed to an alternative which was feasible in the given time frame.

One example from an actual project is provided below.

In one of my projects we were implementing a workflow to automate the approval of new technology projects. As a part of audit requirements, there were many questionnaires that were supposed to be attached with the various online forms. The client absolutely insisted that the questionnaires should be separate web pages and not be treated as an attachment field. However, we did not have the time to implement this in the first version of the product. I negotiated with the client and explained to them that the key for the first version is the business rules that control the workflow. Making online forms out of the questionnaires is merely a nice-to-have feature, and we will provide it in the next release. If we try to accommodate that in this release, then the entire project timeline can be jeopardized. This convinced the client and we came to a middle ground.

4)   Provide an example of how you handled a situation where the development team didn't think it was practical to implement a requirement in the requested time

Answer: In one of my projects there was a requirement to automate general ledger entries. There would be more than ten thousand entries every day, and at the onset, it looked like a requirement that would consume a lot of development time and resources.

The development team equated the daily volume with the amount of work and hence had a lot of resistance to committing to deliver it. I analyzed the entire requirement and realized that just because there are ten thousand general ledger entries a day, it does not mean that there are ten thousand distinct customizations. There were only 4 types of entries and 10 data points underlying each entry. Additionally, the development team was thinking very inefficiently about sourcing data for the implementation. I spoke to them and explained that we can reuse a lot of existing data and can optimize it. The development team also accepted this, and we could move forward with the delivery.

5)   Provide an example of how you handled a situation where the business team proposed requirements which were not feasible in time?

Answer: In one of my projects, the business team insisted on integrating the entry point for two different regulatory systems. This was very convenient and logical from a business perspective, but what the business users did not realize was that these were two different applications built on different technologies and managed by different teams. I realized that request was not practical to be implemented within the given time frame.

Without debating on their request, I tried suggesting alternative options to address the business problem, like having common entry points but keeping the two systems separate from a technical architecture perspective. I slowly made them aware of the feasibility of different alternatives within different time frames, and the client agreed to an alternative which was feasible in the given time frame.

6)   **Provide an example of how you handled a situation where the business team proposed requirements which they didn't agree on among themselves.**

Answer: In situations where there are more than a few business users who didn't agree among themselves and I was running out of time, I let them know the short timeframe and asked them if we could park the issue, have them discuss it offline and let me know the agreed functionality at a later time.

I also tried the approach of taking consensus and then moved forward quickly if there was a majority.

We also established a protocol that there should be only one person that signs off on the requirement. So the user group can debate about it before the sign off but not after sign off. All change requests after sign off used to go as change requests.

For example, in a recent project, I have built an application that caters to multiple lines of businesses. All of them have a common workflow but many of the nuances are different. During requirements discussions, they end up requesting radically different business rules for the same situation. We have appointed a central product owner who knows that we can permit a maximum of 20% customization. We evaluate each customization requirement to check if it's an absolute must-have for the business and use escalations if we feel that it is not.

7) Provide an example of how you handled a situation where the business team provided solutions instead of providing requirements

Answer: This happened very often when the 'business users' had been using the system for a long time and were involved in building it originally. The tendency is to state solutions as requirements. For example, saying "Enhance the ABC upload to add new columns for Australia, Canada and Brazil taxes" when the business need is more like "System should accommodate tax calculations for Australia, Canada, and Brazil."

I requested the business users provide only requirements first as a protocol and politely told them we can always discuss the solutions after the tech team comes back with a proposal. They were hesitant at first and also there was a learning curve, but it worked out fine in the end. The product was much better and requirements capture was very streamlined.

8) Provide an example of a situation where the technical team had a rift with you somewhere in the middle of the project because of unclear requirements

Answer: There was one project where it was about a reporting application with very strict calculation and formatting rules that could not be captured easily in documents. Additionally, the clients would also keep changing their minds. This led to a rift with the development team as they were under severe time pressure and were feeling like they were being pushed into a corner for something they were not responsible for.__When requirements seemed too unclear, I set up a meeting with the development team. Ion the meetings we would go over any terminology or areas in my documentation that they found confusing. I also asked some key members of the technology team to join the requirements discussion so that they felt like a part of the process and would also be able to give me better feedback on how they want to see it documented.

I proposed a half hour every alternate day as an informal meeting to clarify questions. This worked very well and we were able to get back on track as a team.

9) How would you handle a situation where the business users radically changed requirements after a sign off in the middle of development?

Answer: If it's early in the game where too much time/effort has not been spent then it's always good to back track and shelve the project. If it's too far into the game, then the ROI has to be reevaluated with the sunk cost to see if it still makes sense. Alternatively, a phased delivery approach can be suggested that will address the high priority items first and others later, considering the lost time.

10) What were some of the challenges in your project and how have you addressed them?

Losing requirements:

In the initial months, there was a lot of information overkill from various sources. As a result, it was difficult to keep track of requirements. I organized the effort by making sure that we have MOMs (Minutes of the meeting) published after every meeting with a minimum turnaround time of 1 day.

These MOMs were saved in a SharePoint folder for everyone to access. The scope document was based off these MOMs so that the information was not lost. All documents after the initial scope document had very clear traceability (backwards and forwards), so we would never lose track of the bigger picture while working on details

Conflict of opinion amongst SMEs of different departments:

This project involved people from different departments with different priorities. This sometimes made the environment politically charged. We mitigated this by ensuring that we have a solid stakeholder matrix in place with the RACI, escalation paths and exit criteria for each phase clearly spelled out. For any conflict, I first tried to resolve using negotiations and my knowledge of the process. Ninety percent of the conflicts were managed by having conversations. For those that were not, we had a documented escalation path.

Aggressive development cycles:

The development was Agile 6 week sprints and hence could get quite aggressive in terms of timelines. It was a demanding job, and I had to be on top of things all the time. However, being diligent by nature, it was not a problem for me as learning new things and ensuring I give 100% to my job is more important to me at this stage of my life than focusing on getting easy working hours.

Different priorities for different managers:

Being a Waterfall model, it was challenging because of the number of different lines of business involved. Different things were important for different business managers, depending on the nature of their business. However, it was a unified system. As a BA, I had to walk a tightrope to ensure that everyone got the capabilities they required, but it still came out as a unified tool.

There were many steps I took to ensure this which included giving a consistent message of the strategic nature of the endeavors to the team, constantly making sure all stakeholders were on the same page regarding requirements and progress, and keeping the elicitation process very transparent so that people can raise a red flag way ahead of time if they feel something is not working as per their need. I also tried to eliminate silos and encourage more collaborative work.

11)   What are the different personality types of stakeholders you have worked with in the past, and how have you managed them?

Answer: The following are very usual personality types in most projects and also in real life and my suggestions for working with each type is provided below. One has to also note that humans are multidimensional, and the same person may exhibit more than one of the following characteristics based on circumstantial factors.

a)   An SME who really knows everything about the business process

For such a stakeholder, I would
-       Leverage their knowledge as it's a rare quality to find.

-       Build trust by excelling and coming up to speed as fast as possible.

-       Track their success criteria and align common agendas around it.

b)   Disinterested stakeholder

Sometimes people get disinterested in the project because of personal factors or hitting a career wall. If such a person was my key stakeholder, I would use the following techniques:

-       Understand what benefits, motivates, and interests them.

-       Slowly build trust and not be overly aggressive.

-       Try to subtly bring up items in the project that financially or emotionally interest them.

c)   The not so knowledgeable stakeholder

Not all key stakeholders are always well versed with the business side. This might be because of the person's capabilities, interest level, or because they are very new themselves. Sometimes they might be well versed with the business side but might not have a clue on how it translates into a technology product.

With such a stakeholder my strategy would be:

\- Try to provide lots of examples, user stories, and demos of similar solutions.

\- Provide a lot of options at all stages thus preempting their decision making.

d) Overbooked stakeholder

Sometimes your stakeholder might be a very key person and hence always overbooked without much time to spend with you on requirements. In such cases I would use the following strategies:

\- Leverage non-intrusive elicitation techniques so that they don't feel rushed.

\- Book their time only after significant preparation and analysis.

\- Develop abilities to extrapolate information they give in minimum time.

e) The meeting dominator

There are always cases where there is one vocal person who wants to dominate the meeting. With such stakeholders, I would do the following politely:

- Gently facilitate to ensure that everyone gets a chance to speak.

- Have logical and rational points ready in situations where he/she needs to be countered.

- Try to demonstrate how his/her agenda can benefit by having diverse opinions.

12) Name some common issues that happen during requirements gathering and your way of dealing with them.

Answer: The various issues that I have observed in my experience during requirement gathering and my way to mitigate them are:

Insufficient time/input from user - Do a lot of background work before setting up time with busy users. Use non-intrusive elicitation techniques. Raise a red flag early on if there is insufficient input and do not agree for signoff.

Hidden requirements - Best way to mitigate this is to have a lot of examples, scenarios, past results, and possibilities analyzed and share it with the business users to get their opinion.

Conflicting stakeholder opinions – This is a situation where a stakeholder provides conflicting requirements on different occasions. The best way to mitigate this is to document everything, include all relevant people in meetings, record everything as MOM, identify scope and assumptions early on, get formal sign offs.

Constant change in requirements - Finalize and adhere to rigid change management policies and set right expectations in case of change. Have a strong version control and track changes and history for all documents.

12. Dissecting Projects on Your Résumé

Your interview and the answers you provide are closely related to your résumé. Your résumé is the single most critical aspect of getting a foot in the door. Additionally, remember that most interviews are never longer than 1 hour per person, so there is only enough time to focus on your résumé and find out whether you are a good fit.

That being said, a lot of the answers we have provided in this book *must be customized by you* based on the projects you have listed on your résumé. However, before you customize the answers, you need to have a visceral understanding of the projects listed on your résumé. Hence, we would advise you to make 'project flash cards' for at least the projects spanning the last 5 years on your résumé.

A project flash card lists out the most important business and technology summary points about a given project and your role in it. This serves as a good cheat sheet for you to get familiar with your talking points.

Most interviews start with the interviewer asking you to give an elevator talk on some of your recent projects. It is often said that the first five minutes are when most of the decisions are made. The rest of the interview is usually spent validating the decision made from that first impression. It is thus critical for you to put your best foot forward when you provide the project overview.

We have created a sample 'project flash card' for a project which will help you to create your own. The flashcard can be found below:

What does the company do? Fannie Mae is the leading source of residential mortgage credit in the U.S. secondary market; it is supporting today's economic recovery and helping to build a sustainable housing system.

What was the business problem? Fannie Mae was handling and restructuring millions of dollars' worth of loans each minute but the systems they used were homemade Excel reporting tools. This was initially managed by a huge team of loan processing analysts who used to manually update every single loan detail and restructure them which resulted in inefficiencies, mainly slow processing time caused by the loan processing team updating and restructuring loans, periodic reporting since the team reported every month end, and inaccuracies due to manual reporting.

What was the objective of your project? *The leadership wanted us to build an OBIEE system that would: Automate the process of restructuring delinquent loans to reduce the number of foreclosures that we were going through and align the process with regulatory standards like HUD Hamp guidelines.*

- *Report key mortgage metrics on a daily basis like mortgage installments, balance, modified interest rate and term of the loan, and LPI dates. This system offered significant benefits like automation of millions of mortgage reporting, restructuring data, reduced processing time, and improved data accuracy.*

What were the key challenges? *The main challenge was a lack of time. There had been several delays in the early part of the project which resulted in a very compressed time frame to complete quality assurance. The second challenge was that the requirements document was incomplete, since the BA had changed in the middle of the project and continuity in the documents was an issue. Finally, there were a lot of data-related details that resulted in intense manual testing.*

What results did the project achieve? *The project went live in 18 months. We achieved great results. The transition to an*

Oracle-based system reduced processing time by 50%. For example, before the system went live, it would take 10 team members to update the Excel reporting every 24 hours. After transition, the Oracle interface automatically updated reports every 12 hours without human intervention. The system also increased accuracy by 60%.

13. In Conclusion

As you've learned throughout this text, you need to build a strong case that you are the best fit for the job. In doing so, you need to ensure that you:

- Link key points in your résumé to the job being offered.

- Avoid negativity of any kind, such as talking bad about a past employer, manager, or even yourself.

- Breathe life into the interview by using examples from your experience, and prove that you have the right attitude and team spirit.

- Drive the interview to your strong points, avoiding a discussion concerning your weaker areas.

We wish you the best of luck going out and getting the job you so deserve. We are here to help, so please feel free to give us a call or send us an email at **info@kuebikoglobal.com**. In addition to online training, we also offer sample résumé and mock interview packages.

Note to reader: We would love to hear your feedback. Please send your comments, criticisms, billing inquiries, and suggestions for future updates to **info@kuebikoglobal.com**.

Sign up to receive our exclusive introductory gift (a $15 value) by sending us an email. We will send you a powerful, highly-customized, 200-slide PPT toolkit that contains detailed slides for any kind of management preparation. Using this, you will never have to work on a PowerPoint slide from scratch again. Plus, you will never miss out on new tutorials, tips, and updates!

Kuebiko Global provides innovative online training and career support programs in a variety of information technology management areas and associated business operations. We specialize in providing practical, real-world knowledge and skills that are required for success in the modern IT industry. Our experienced professionals take inspiration from "Kuebiko", the Japanese god of wisdom.

We offer training and consulting, coupled with industry domain knowledge, in various areas of the techno-functional space, including business systems analysis, project management, quality assurance, technology recruitment, and niche software packages. Our training services are ideal for working professionals looking to diversify their skill sets, college students seeking to start their careers and companies looking for a training partner.

Thank you,
The Kuebiko Global

Made in the USA
Monee, IL
06 October 2020